The Man Who Made the Shadows Dance: John Logie Baird

Michael Webster

Published by Michael Webster, 2025.

While every precaution has been taken in the preparation of this book, the publisher assumes no responsibility for errors or omissions, or for damages resulting from the use of the information contained herein.

THE MAN WHO MADE THE SHADOWS DANCE: JOHN LOGIE BAIRD

First edition. December 21, 2025.

Copyright © 2025 Michael Webster.

ISBN: 979-8233924965

Written by Michael Webster.

Table of Contents

....1

Introduction: The Man Who Made the Shadows Dance........................2

Chapter 1: The Formative Years (1888–1915)..4

1.1 Birth, Family, and the Victorian Era Context in Helensburgh, Scotland. 5

1.2 Early Education and the Influence of Science and Engineering.......7

1.3 University Studies at Glasgow and the West of Scotland Technical College. 9

1.4 Early Inventions and Mechanical Experiments (e.g., the self-propelled trolley)..11

1.5 Interruption of Studies and the Impact of World War I................13

Chapter 2: Wartime and Commercial Diversions (1915–1922).........15

2.1 Attempts to Enlist and the Impact of Chronic Ill-Health on his Career. 16

2.2 Early Business Ventures: From Jam to Soggy Socks (Baird's unique rubber boot venture). 18

2.3 The Failure of the 'Baird Undersocks' Company and Financial Setbacks..20

2.4 Moving to Trinidad and Tobago and the Attempt to Grow Bananas. 22

2.5 Return to Britain and the Initial Shift in Focus towards Wireless Technology. 24

Chapter 3: The Theoretical Foundation of Vision (1922–1924)........26

3.1 The Concept of Image Scanning: Precursors and Theorical Models....................27

3.2 Setting up the First Laboratory in Hastings and the Lack of Funding....................29

3.3 The Role of the Nipkow Disc and the Principles of Mechanical Scanning....................31

3.4 Initial Apparatus: Scraps, Sealing Wax, and the Tea Chest....................33

3.5 The Vision: Transmitting a Moving Image, not just Static Pictures....................35

Chapter 4: The First Breakthrough (1924–1926)....................37

4.1 The First Successful Transmission of an Outline Image (The Maltese Cross)....................38

4.2 Media Attention and the Move to Soho, London, to Find Investors....................40

4.3 The Critical Day: January 26, 1926 – The Public Demonstration to the Royal Institution....................42

4.4 The Demonstration of 'Televisor': Transmission of a Recognisable Human Face (Siki)....................44

4.5 Technical Specifications of the First Operational System (30-line resolution)....................46

Chapter 5: Commercialisation and Public Exposure (1926–1928)...48

5.1 Formation of the Baird Television Development Company (BTDC)....................49

5.2 The Importance of Shortwave Radio and the First Experiments with Broadcast....................51

5.3 Development of the Phonovision System (Recording Television). 53

5.4 Public Demonstrations at Selfridges and Other Major Department Stores. 55

5.5 Growing Media Rivalry and Skepticism from the Scientific Establishment. 57

Chapter 6: The Dawn of Global Television (1928–1929) 59

6.1 The Historic Transatlantic Transmission from London to New York. 60

6.2 The First Outdoor Television Broadcast (The Epsom Derby). 62

6.3 Experiments with Colour Television (The Trichromatic Method). 64

6.4 The First Demonstration of Stereoscopic (3D) Television. 66

6.5 International Expansion: Licensing and Demonstrations in Germany and the USA. 68

Chapter 7: The BBC and the Zenith of Mechanical TV (1929–1932) 70

7.1 Collaboration with the British Broadcasting Corporation (BBC) for Trial Broadcasts. 71

7.2 Installation of Baird Equipment at the BBC's Savoy Hill Studios. 73

7.3 Broadcast Schedules and the Content of Early 30-Line Television Programs. 75

7.4 The Launch of Commercial Televisors for Home Use. 77

7.5 The Consolidation of Mechanical Television as the World Standard 79

Chapter 8: The Shadow of Electronic Television (1932–1935) 81

8.1 The Financial and Technical Troubles of the Baird Company 82

8.2 The Growing Threat from EMI/Marconi and the Electronic (Cathode Ray Tube) System 85

8.3 Baird's Response: Developing Intermediate Film (IF) and High-Definition Mechanical Systems 88

8.4 The Failure to Achieve a Viable High-Definition Mechanical Standard (240 lines) 90

8.5 Government Intervention: The Appointment of the Television Committee 92

8.6 The Initial Planning and Preparations for the Alexandra Palace Trial 94

Chapter 9: The Alexandra Palace Trials and Defeat (1936–1937) 96

9.1 The Decision to Hold a Side-by-Side Comparison Trial by the BBC 97

9.2 The Rival Systems: Baird's Improved Mechanical/IF System vs. the EMI-Marconi Electronic System 99

9.3 Technical Differences and Operational Challenges of the Two Systems 101

9.4 The Government's Decision to Adopt the EMI-Marconi System 103

9.5 The Immediate Aftermath and the End of the 30-Line Broadcasts 105

Chapter 10: Private Innovation During World War II (1937–1945) 107

10.1 Baird's Shift Away from Commercial Broadcast towards Specialized Innovation 108

10.2 Continuous Work on High-Definition Colour Television (The Telechrome Tube) 110

10.3 The Development of Advanced Theatre Television (The Projector System) 112

10.4 The Impact of the Second World War on Television Development in Britain 114

10.5 Baird's Final Patented Inventions and Technical Documents from the War Years 116

Chapter 11: Personal Life, Health, and Family (1900–1946) 118

11.1 Marriage to Margaret Albu and the Dynamics of Family Life. 119

11.2 Life in London and the Challenges of Chronic Illness (Tuberculosis) 121

11.3 Financial Struggles and the Stress of Perpetual Innovation 123

11.4 The Public Perception of Baird and his Relationship with the Press 125

11.5 Baird as a Mentor and the Team of Engineers Who Worked Closely with Him 127

Chapter 12: Legacy and Final Assessments (1946–Present) 129

12.1 Death in Bexhill-on-Sea, Sussex, and the Immediate Tributes 130

12.2 The Debate: Mechanical Genius vs. Electronic Failure 132

12.3 Post-War Recognition and the Resumption of British Television 134

12.4 Preserving the Artifacts: Televisors and Phonovision Records in Museums 136

12.5 Baird's Enduring Place in History as the Inventor of the First Working Television 138

Conclusion 140

The Singular Contribution: Television's Foundational Architect 141

The Persistence of the Pioneer: Proving the Concept 144

Final Assessment: Triumph of the Spirit 146

Appendix 148

List of Key Patents (1923–1946) 149

Glossary of Technical Terms 152

Timeline of Major Milestones 155

Bibliographical Notes and Source Suggestions 157

The Man Who Made the Shadows Dance: John Logie Baird

The Epic Story of John Logie Baird, the Man Who Invented Television—And Was Written Out of History

Introduction: The Man Who Made the Shadows Dance

In the history of innovation, few figures embody the mixture of genius, relentless struggle, and bittersweet fate quite like **John Logie Baird**. Mention his name today, and you might receive a vague nod—a forgotten footnote in the whirlwind story of the moving image. Yet, it was this frail, often penniless Scottish engineer who, in a dimly lit London laboratory in 1926, accomplished what had been deemed impossible: the first successful transmission of a true, recognizable television image. He made the shadows dance.

Baird's life was a testament to sheer, obsessive willpower, played out against a constant battle with ill health. Before he was the father of television, he was a curious inventor, his early career marked by a series of eccentric failures, from his famous attempts to create diamond-making machinery to his profitable but ultimately abandoned scheme for producing foot-warming socks. These anecdotes are not mere footnotes; they reveal the restless, practical mind that eventually settled on the single, grand challenge of his age: seeing by wireless.

The world Baird sought to conquer was one of wires and radio waves, and his solution was elegantly mechanical. Using rotating cardboard discs, perforated with a spiral pattern—the **Nipkow Disc**—and highly sensitive selenium cells, he built a system that could break down a face into thirty flickering lines of light and reconstruct it instantly at a distance. It was rudimentary, requiring the use of glaring neon lamps and often rendering images small enough to require a lens, but it worked. His public demonstration to the Royal Institution fundamentally changed the technological landscape forever, launching the world's first public television service.

This book is more than a technical biography; it is an exploration of a pioneering age. We delve into the fierce, cutthroat **race for television**, detailing Baird's corporate battles, the financial schemes that kept his company afloat, and his constant struggle to keep pace with the concurrent, rapid advances in electronic technology being developed by giants like EMI-Marconi. His triumphs—achieving colour television, transatlantic transmission, and stereoscopic vision—were monumental. Yet, his eventual heartbreak, when the BBC ultimately abandoned his mechanical system in favor of the electronic standard, forms the central tragedy of his narrative.

Through detailed analysis of his numerous patents, personal correspondence, and contemporary interviews, we explore the extraordinary cultural impact of television's birth and how Baird laid the groundwork for the medium that would define the twentieth century. From his early days of poverty to his final, brilliant attempts to perfect an all-electronic colour system (the **Telechrome**), this work traces the full scope of a genius who dared to look past the radio receiver and envision a world united by pictures in the air. Turn the page to begin the story of the man who gave us the power to see beyond the horizon.

Chapter 1: The Formative Years (1888–1915)

1.1 Birth, Family, and the Victorian Era Context in Helensburgh, Scotland.

The world John Logie Baird entered on August 13, 1888, was one poised on the cusp of dizzying technological transformation, yet still firmly rooted in the moral and intellectual framework of late Victorian Scotland. His birthplace, Helensburgh, was not the gritty industrial heartland often associated with Scottish invention, but a serene, affluent burgh on the north shore of the Firth of Clyde, offering fresh air, scenic views, and a comfortable distance from the smoke of Glasgow. It was a place designed for successful middle and upper-class families, providing an ideal environment for contemplative thought and focused study, away from the immediate pressures of industry. Baird's family background contributed significantly to his later character: one part rooted in spiritual duty, the other in intellectual curiosity. His father, the Reverend John Baird, was the minister of the West Parish Church, a figure of considerable local standing and moral authority. His mother, Jessie Inglis, was the orphaned niece of a prominent Glasgow shipbuilding family, the McLeans. This duality—the clerical severity of the manse combined with the financial security and industrial legacy of the Glasgow shipyards—provided a unique backdrop to his childhood.

The manse itself was a hive of activity, both intellectual and social. The Reverend Baird was a respected community leader, and the family's life revolved around the strict but nurturing tenets of Presbyterianism. This upbringing instilled in the young John a deep, almost puritanical work ethic, a belief in the relentless pursuit of difficult goals, and a profound seriousness that often masked his innovative fire. His health, however, was an immediate and constant complication. Born into a time when endemic diseases like tuberculosis were still rampant, Baird was afflicted from childhood by a persistent fragility. This poor constitution meant he was often shielded from the robust activities of his peers and forced inward, finding solace and intellectual adventure in books, experiments, and solitary observation. It was this enforced introspection, perhaps more than any formal schooling, that nurtured the intense focus required for his future work. While the world outside Helensburgh was characterized by the booming global reach of the British Empire and the dizzying speed of industrial advancement—from the telephone and electric light to the first practical automobiles—Baird's early life was marked by the quiet, disciplined rhythm of the Scottish manse.

The Victorian culture surrounding him was one that revered invention and the application of science to human problems. Figures like James Clerk Maxwell, Lord Kelvin, and Alexander Graham Bell—all with strong Scottish ties—were national heroes. Their work established a powerful intellectual current that elevated engineering and physics from mere trades to noble, intellectual pursuits. Though Baird would eventually become known for mechanical solutions at a time when electronics were emerging, his initial inspiration drew from this late Victorian tradition of resourceful, hand-built, functional ingenuity. The atmosphere was ripe for a boy with a predisposition for tinkering. The long, dark Scottish winters and the seclusion of the manse provided the perfect environment for a scientifically inclined child to pore over instruction manuals and take apart domestic devices, beginning a lifelong habit of using whatever materials were immediately at hand to solve vast, conceptual problems. This early environment, far from the industrial noise, refined his focus and set the stage for the single-minded obsession that would eventually define his career. His physical limitations became, paradoxically, the source of his intense mental concentration, directing his energy away from physical labor and towards the daunting, abstract challenge of transmitting sight across distances.

1.2 Early Education and the Influence of Science and Engineering.

Baird's formal education began, as was common for children of his social standing, at the local academy, Helensburgh School. The school provided a solid grounding in the classics and mathematics, but it was outside the prescribed curriculum where Baird's true passions ignited. From an early age, he demonstrated an almost compulsive need to understand how things worked and, more importantly, how to make them work better. Unlike many of his peers who were content to consume the new technology of the age, Baird was determined to be a producer, a creator. His mother and father, though perhaps sometimes perplexed by his endless experiments, were supportive of his scientific bent, often indulging his requests for tools, chemicals, and electrical components. The most significant early influence, however, was his intellectual curiosity combined with the practical, hands-on application of engineering principles.

The late nineteenth century saw the widespread popularisation of electricity and magnetism, and the young Baird quickly became adept at manipulating these new forces. His room, and later various sheds and outbuildings, quickly transformed into private laboratories. This was an education in practical science, learned through trial and error, often resulting in minor explosions, smoky rooms, and the occasional electrical shock. One of his earliest and most illustrative exploits involved establishing a basic telephone exchange to connect his house to those of a few friends nearby. This was not merely a simple wire connection; it required the resourcefulness to scavenge materials, the skill to build or adapt the necessary components (transmitters, receivers, and signaling mechanisms), and the persistence to maintain the delicate wiring over considerable distances. The success of this homemade system was a foundational moment, demonstrating his ability to conceive of a complex communications network and execute it entirely with limited resources—a skill that would later be central to the development of his mechanical television apparatus.

The intellectual atmosphere of the time also provided a constant supply of inspiration. Popular science magazines and journals, widely read by the aspirational middle class, frequently featured articles discussing the cutting edge of invention, particularly in wireless communication and the emerging field of image transmission. While the theoretical work on television had been articulated by figures like Paul Nipkow decades earlier, the practical realization remained elusive. Baird absorbed these articles, not as passive reader but as a challenge to his own ingenuity. His focus gravitated toward engineering, rather than pure physics, valuing functional mechanics over abstract theory. This preference would be both his greatest strength and his ultimate professional limitation. It gave him the determination to build a working model first, regardless of the elegance of the underlying science, but later made his system vulnerable to the theoretically superior electronic solutions developed by rivals.

His early school years, therefore, were less about academic achievement in the conventional sense and more about forging a deep, personal relationship with technology. He learned the harsh reality of engineering: that theory often collides violently with physical materials, and that success is usually found in the messy, painstaking process of iteration and refinement. This period solidified his identity as a determined inventor, someone who saw a problem not as an obstacle, but as a technical puzzle demanding a unique, resource-bound solution. The Scottish education system provided the structure, but the real influence was the spirit of scientific enterprise that permeated the age, encouraging the young man to aim his inventive sights high, toward seemingly impossible goals.

1.3 University Studies at Glasgow and the West of Scotland Technical College.

The progression to higher education was a natural step for the intellectually curious Baird, and in 1906, he began his studies at the Glasgow and West of Scotland Technical College, later known as the Royal Technical College. This institution was a powerhouse of practical engineering, focusing on applied sciences directly relevant to Scotland's massive industrial output—shipbuilding, heavy machinery, and electrical power generation. This environment perfectly suited Baird's pragmatic and hands-on approach to problem-solving. While he later enrolled concurrently at the University of Glasgow, his time at the Technical College proved to be the more defining experience, emphasizing the mechanics and practical physics that would form the basis of his later work. The curriculum immersed him in the principles of mechanical power, hydraulics, and, crucially, electrical engineering, providing the rigorous foundation necessary to transition from backyard tinkering to serious invention.

The contrast between the quiet intellectualism of Helensburgh and the vibrant, often brutal, industrial reality of Glasgow was stark. Baird was exposed to the cutting edge of industrial practice, seeing how complex systems were designed, manufactured, and implemented at scale. This was the era of massive steam turbines and nascent high-tension electrical grids. The classes were populated by men who would go on to manage factories and design bridges, instilling a culture of practical competence. Baird excelled in the aspects that appealed to his inventive mind, particularly in the labs where he could directly manipulate apparatus and conduct experiments. However, his studies were frequently hampered by his chronic ill health, a recurring theme that would plague his entire life. The demands of the rigorous curriculum, coupled with the necessity of living in the colder, more humid environment of the city, often led to periods of sickness that forced him to interrupt his attendance.

Despite these interruptions, the core knowledge acquired in Glasgow was indispensable. He studied under professors who were themselves contributing to the rapid advances in electrical technology, learning about alternating current, radio waves, and the principles of electromagnetic transmission. It was during this time that he would have been exposed in a formal setting to the theories of photoelectricity—the idea that light could be converted into an electric current—and the mechanical scanning techniques proposed by Paul Nipkow. While his later work on television would be driven by relentless practical experimentation, the conceptual jump from theory to execution was only made possible by the comprehensive theoretical framework he absorbed during his university years. He did not invent television in a vacuum; he began his work armed with a sophisticated understanding of the physical limitations and possibilities inherent in late-nineteenth and early-twentieth-century technology.

The completion of his professional qualifications led him to an apprenticeship at the Albion Motor Car Company in Glasgow. This experience was vital, providing him with intimate knowledge of precision engineering, the practical use of machine tools, and the importance of tolerances—skills essential for building the delicate, fast-moving parts of the mechanical television system. His apprenticeship was another period marred by health issues, but it served its purpose, transforming him from a theoretically informed student into a fully practical engineer. This dual education—the applied physics from the college and the precision mechanics from the factory floor—provided Baird with the perfect, albeit unusual, skill set for his eventual life's work: he knew the science of electrical signals and the practical mechanics of how to manipulate physical material to capture, transmit, and display those signals.

1.4 Early Inventions and Mechanical Experiments (e.g., the self-propelled trolley).

The period following his formal education and factory apprenticeship marked Baird's transition from student to full-time, if unconventional, inventor. Having acquired the technical skills, he now sought practical problems to solve, often motivated by either a sense of social usefulness or, perhaps more often, a need for a viable commercial enterprise. This era, stretching from his early twenties until the war, is characterized by a dizzying array of experiments and minor commercial failures, demonstrating a boundless, if sometimes unfocused, ingenuity. The unifying thread through these varied projects was a commitment to mechanical and electrical solutions, usually executed with a minimal budget and maximal resourcefulness, reflecting his Scottish pragmatism and his persistent lack of capital.

One of his most illustrative, and almost comedic, early inventions was the self-propelled trolley, a device he designed to transport goods locally. While the concept sounds mundane, its execution involved adapting existing mechanical principles in novel ways. The goal was to create a cheap, reliable, automated delivery vehicle, prefiguring modern logistics solutions by decades. This project, like many others, ultimately faltered not due to a failure in concept but because of his chronic inability to manage the commercialization process or sustain the physical effort required for execution. He was, fundamentally, an inventor and tinkerer, easily distracted by the next technical challenge, and ill-suited to the drudgery of business management and marketing.

Another significant, though commercially doomed, venture was a method for manufacturing cheap, durable diamonds. This was based on the premise that intense pressure and heat could mimic geological processes. Using a rudimentary apparatus, he attempted to create synthetic stones, a risky and dangerous experiment conducted with minimal safety measures. The result, predictably, was a series of small explosions and no viable diamonds, but the episode highlights his willingness to tackle fundamentally difficult problems in physics and chemistry using nothing more than brute-force mechanical ingenuity. His attempts to generate large quantities of electricity via a simple, cheap battery system also consumed considerable time and energy, again demonstrating an underlying desire to democratize or simplify access to technology, a goal that would reappear with his vision of the Televisor as a household object.

These pre-television experiments were invaluable as training grounds. They taught him the hard lessons of prototyping: the instability of certain components, the unforgiving nature of mechanical tolerances, and the critical importance of a stable power source. They also reinforced his methodology—to isolate the core physical principle and build a working, often crude, model around it, using whatever materials were available. This 'sealing wax and string' approach, born of necessity, would later become the defining aesthetic of his first television apparatus. The failures of the trolley, the diamond machine, and the battery project were not wasted time; they were the essential education in mechanical and entrepreneurial survival that prepared him for the decade-long struggle to bring television to the world. He learned how to persist when prototypes failed and how to extract the maximum functional utility from the minimum investment of resources, a quality that would prove essential when he finally focused his attention on the daunting challenge of transmitting images.

1.5 Interruption of Studies and the Impact of World War I.

The shadow that fell across Europe in August 1914 fundamentally altered the trajectory of John Logie Baird's life, as it did for his entire generation. While he had been attempting to establish himself as an inventor and entrepreneur in the years immediately preceding the conflict, the outbreak of the First World War brought an end to his relatively unfettered experimentation and severely curtailed his attempts at commercial success. The war effort demanded that all industrial and inventive capacity be channeled toward military necessity, making materials scarce, investment capital non-existent for non-essential projects, and scientific personnel highly sought after for military applications. For Baird, the impact was both personal and professional.

Like many young men, Baird attempted to enlist in the armed forces. However, his lifelong history of poor health, particularly his recurring bronchial and general frailty, immediately disqualified him from military service. The constant illness and weak constitution that had shaped his early life now, ironically, exempted him from the horrors of the trenches, but this inability to serve carried a profound emotional weight. At a time when service was a moral and social imperative, being barred from duty due to physical failings was a source of frustration and, perhaps, a sense of inadequacy that further spurred his drive for achievement in the civilian sphere.

As a qualified engineer with technical expertise, he found work at the Clyde Valley Electrical Power Company, performing essential services vital to the wartime industrial machine. This employment provided a stable income during a period of intense economic upheaval and, perhaps more significantly, gave him access to advanced electrical equipment and practical knowledge of power generation and transmission on a massive scale. This exposure to high-voltage, large-scale electrical infrastructure would later inform his understanding of the powerful signal processing required for broadcasting images across distances. The war, therefore, while an interruption of his personal ambitions, served as a grim, accelerated technical apprenticeship in real-world, high-stakes engineering.

However, the war's overall effect was to push him away from the industrialized heartland. The relentless stress, the long hours, and the polluted air of industrial Glasgow during wartime intensified his respiratory problems. By 1915, his health deteriorated to such an extent that continuing his work became untenable. This physical crisis forced a major life decision: he had to leave the cold, damp, industrial environment of Scotland to survive. The decision was not just a flight from poor health but a retreat from the world of conventional engineering, which was now fully focused on war. This critical period of interruption provided the necessary pause, the psychological space, and the physical mandate to turn his focus from minor commercial distractions and wartime electrical work toward a completely different path. He would soon abandon the heavy engineering of the Clyde for the warmer climates and the abstract pursuit of his greatest challenge. The war years, by eliminating alternatives and exacerbating his poor health, inadvertently steered John Logie Baird toward the single-minded pursuit of an idea that had been gestating since his early days of tinkering: the conquest of visible light and its transmission through the air.

Chapter 2: Wartime and Commercial Diversions (1915–1922)

2.1 Attempts to Enlist and the Impact of Chronic Ill-Health on his Career.

The commencement of the Great War in 1914 cast a long and pervasive shadow over the lives of all young men in Britain, and John Logie Baird, despite his inventive and intellectual leanings, was no exception to the national call to arms. His upbringing in the patriotic and morally rigorous environment of the Scottish manse likely instilled in him a keen sense of duty and the desire to contribute to the war effort. The initial rush of patriotic fervour saw millions lining up to enlist, and Baird, then twenty-six, felt the moral obligation to join them. However, his physical reality was a profound barrier. From his earliest childhood, Baird had suffered from persistent ill-health, characterized by chronic respiratory weakness and frequent bouts of sickness, likely a form of tuberculosis or chronic bronchitis that left him perpetually frail and susceptible to the cold and damp. These conditions, which had hampered his university studies and complicated his factory apprenticeship, now presented an unyielding obstacle to military service.

His attempts to enlist were met with immediate and definitive rejection by the military medical boards. While the army was often willing to overlook minor physical deficiencies during the massive recruitment drives, Baird's condition was deemed severe enough to render him completely unfit for even non-combatant roles. This rejection had a complex and deep impact on his nascent career and his personal psychology. On one hand, it spared him from the brutalizing experience of the Western Front, preserving his life and health for his future pioneering work. On the other, the rejection during a period of intense national self-sacrifice led to a sense of frustration and, arguably, a deep-seated need for compensatory achievement. He had been rejected by the traditional path of male duty and heroism; he would now seek a different, equally transformative form of service to humanity through invention.

Temporarily, he contributed to the war machine by taking up a position at the Clyde Valley Electrical Power Company, a role that utilized his skills as an engineer to maintain the vital power grid fueling wartime industries. While this work provided stability and relevant technical experience, it was far from the kind of pioneering invention that truly motivated him. The industrial environment, however, continued to take its toll on his weak lungs. The sheer physical stress of the long shifts, combined with the unavoidable exposure to the soot and coal dust of wartime Glasgow, severely exacerbated his chronic chest problems. By 1915, his health reached a point of crisis, making the continuation of heavy industrial work impossible. Doctors were unequivocal: he needed to seek a cleaner, drier climate, or risk permanent and fatal decline. This medical necessity marked the definitive end of his engineering career in Scotland.

The enforced withdrawal from conventional employment, triggered by the war and his poor health, proved to be an unexpected turning point. It removed him from the established, predictable world of employment and threw him into an almost desperate search for a means of living that was independent, non-strenuous, and financially rewarding—a challenge that only an entrepreneurial inventor could solve. His rejection from the military, therefore, did not result in idleness but in an intense redirection of his prodigious, restless energy toward a series of increasingly idiosyncratic commercial ventures, all aimed at achieving the financial independence and physical freedom necessary to pursue his true love: invention. The need to find a means of making money that did not involve cold weather or physical exertion became the primary, overriding driver of his life in the years immediately following the initial stage of the war.

2.2 Early Business Ventures: From Jam to Soggy Socks (Baird's unique rubber boot venture).

With his health dictating an immediate shift away from traditional engineering, Baird plunged into a series of eccentric commercial ventures that characterized his entrepreneurial period. This phase of his life, stretching from 1916 to the early 1920s, reveals a man struggling to find his footing, applying an engineer's logic to everyday consumer problems with frequently disastrous results. The transition was driven by a need for quick, non-physical income and reflected his resourceful but naive approach to business. He had the genius of an inventor but lacked the cold pragmatism of a successful marketer or industrialist.

One of his earliest, though less remembered, forays into commerce was a brief involvement in the **jam industry** in Scotland. The logistics of food production and distribution were a complete contrast to his electrical expertise. While the precise details of this venture are hazy, it epitomizes his willingness to try anything, applying his analytical mind to maximize efficiency in production, only to be confounded by the realities of supply chains and consumer tastes. It was a short-lived distraction, quickly abandoned when the next, more compelling, idea struck him: solving the persistent problem of cold and damp feet.

This next venture became the famous, or perhaps infamous, **Baird Undersocks** or rubber boot socks enterprise. The idea originated from a genuine observation of a common problem faced by working-class people in damp climates: how to keep feet dry and warm inside ill-fitting or leaky rubber boots and shoes. Baird's innovative solution was not merely a thick sock, but a unique, disposable sock lining impregnated with boracic powder, designed to be worn inside gumboots. The lining absorbed moisture, kept the feet dry, and was insulated by the rubber. It was a clever application of material science and thermal insulation, turning a common discomfort into a specialized niche product.

He established the small-scale manufacturing operation in Rothesay on the Isle of Bute, an environment chosen partly for his health and partly for its lower operating costs. His business strategy was typical of his resourcefulness: he sought out cheap manufacturing space, secured supplies on credit, and used his charm and technical acumen to persuade small-scale investors to back the product. The initial production runs involved Baird himself overseeing the rudimentary machinery, a task which inevitably pushed his fragile health to the limit. The marketing, however, was where his engineering mind failed to connect with the consumer. He advertised the product on its technical merits—its superior absorbency and insulation—but struggled to create a recognizable brand identity or effective distribution network beyond local chemists and general stores.

For a brief period, the idea took off, primarily because it offered a cheap, ingenious solution to a pervasive problem. He experienced a burst of minor financial success, the first tangible wealth he had earned from his own inventive effort. This temporary flourishing of the 'soggy socks' business was important not for the product itself, but because it confirmed his belief that he could, indeed, generate wealth through his own unique ideas, independently of established industry. It was a taste of success that reinforced his identity as an inventor-entrepreneur, a necessary intermediate step before he tackled the monumental challenge of sight transmission. The venture, despite its eventual failure, was a crucial lesson in commercial reality, tempering his pure inventive idealism with the harsh realities of the marketplace.

2.3 The Failure of the 'Baird Undersocks' Company and Financial Setbacks.

The initial, fleeting success of the Baird Undersocks Company, built on a clever concept and low overheads, soon ran aground on the unforgiving shoals of commercial reality. The failure of this venture, like the others that preceded it, was not attributable to a lack of ingenuity on Baird's part, but rather to a combination of his fundamental unsuitability for sustained business management, undercapitalization, and the recurring nemesis of his life: crippling ill-health. The period from 1918 to 1919 saw the slow, painful dissolution of the company, leaving Baird financially depleted and physically exhausted.

The technical genius behind the sock—the specialized material and the insulating properties—could not overcome the logistical and marketing challenges of mass production. Scaling up the operation proved impossible without significant outside investment, which Baird was unable to secure on a sustainable basis. Distribution became a nightmare; his efforts were localized, and he lacked the network or the capital to push the product into national retail chains. Furthermore, the product itself, being somewhat niche and disposable, required constant manufacturing output and inventory management, tasks that detracted heavily from Baird's true passion for invention and experimentation. He found the day-to-day grind of managing payroll, suppliers, and customer complaints utterly soul-destroying and draining of his limited physical energy.

The most critical factor in the company's downfall was, once again, his health. The constant demand of overseeing the small factory, coupled with the stress of financial anxiety, led to a severe physical relapse. The damp climate of Rothesay, chosen in part for its lower cost of living, was still too harsh for his lungs. He found himself too ill to personally manage the operations, and without his constant, intense oversight, the rudimentary business structure quickly crumbled. The limited capital reserves were exhausted by production costs and the necessary overheads, and soon he was forced to liquidate the assets, leaving him personally liable for debts and back at square one, but with an added burden of failure.

The financial setbacks were crushing. All the modest profits and small investments secured from his earlier ventures had vanished. This period of intense commercial failure instilled in him a deeper understanding of the unforgiving nature of the financial world, a world he desperately needed to master if his future, grander inventions were ever to succeed. More profoundly, the failure led to a severe bout of depression and a feeling of aimlessness. His health crisis meant he could not be an engineer, and his financial failure suggested he could not be a businessman. He was a brilliant inventor trapped in a frail body with an empty bank account.

This low point forced a radical decision. Medical advice was now insistent: he must move to a genuinely tropical climate to save his life. The failure of the undersocks company, therefore, was the final, decisive push that severed his ties to the familiar life of Scotland and launched him toward the far reaches of the globe, seeking a desperate cure for his body and a new, non-stressful means of subsistence. His next venture would be as distant from electrical engineering as possible—an attempt to find health and quiet prosperity in the agrarian life of the Caribbean.

2.4 Moving to Trinidad and Tobago and the Attempt to Grow Bananas.

In 1919, seeking a final reprieve from his persistent ill-health and the unrelenting damp of Britain, John Logie Baird embarked on the most drastic geographical and professional shift of his life: a voyage to the tropics of Trinidad and Tobago. This move was not driven by any new inventive or commercial spark, but solely by medical necessity. His physical constitution was failing rapidly, and the doctor's prescription was simple and urgent: flee to a warm, dry climate where the air would ease his lungs and the pace of life would reduce his stress. He arrived in Port of Spain with little more than his savings from the liquidated undersocks company, a profound weariness, and the determination to find an utterly simple means of supporting himself that required minimal physical or mental strain.

The cultural shock must have been immense. The disciplined, Presbyterian routine of a Scottish manse and the smoky industrial reality of Glasgow were replaced by the languid, tropical heat, the vibrant colours, and the entirely different social rhythm of the Caribbean. He settled near the coastal town of Port-of-Spain and attempted to establish himself as a **fruit grower**, specifically focusing on bananas and, briefly, dabbling in sugar production. This venture was perhaps the most anomalous period of his adult life, placing the mechanical engineer in the role of a colonial planter, a world away from dynamos and vacuum tubes.

Baird approached this new task with the same characteristic analytical intensity he applied to engineering. He studied the soil, the climate, and the optimal conditions for growth, attempting to streamline the agricultural process with the mind of a system designer. However, agriculture proved as frustrating as his previous commercial enterprises, though for entirely different reasons. He was battling not with electrical resistance or mechanical failure, but with the unpredictable forces of nature—insect blights, tropical storms, and the vast logistics of shipping perishable produce across the Atlantic. He was fundamentally unsuited to the patient, slow rhythm of farming. His mind was wired for instantaneous electrical signaling and the dynamic creation of complex devices, not for waiting months for a crop to mature.

The experience in Trinidad provided little financial gain and even less intellectual stimulation. He realized quickly that the manual labour, despite the warmth, was too strenuous, and the challenges of managing local labour and negotiating shipping contracts were as taxing as any business in Britain. The great advantage, however, was the reprieve for his health. The constant warmth and dry air offered a temporary and blessed alleviation of his chronic chest symptoms, allowing his body a period of recovery that was essential for his survival. This physical stabilisation was the single positive outcome of his tropical exile.

Crucially, the sheer boredom of the agrarian life provided the mental space necessary for his true vocation to resurface. Isolated from the immediate pressures of the British engineering scene and lacking a satisfying physical outlet, his thoughts inevitably turned back to the great, unsolved communication problem of the age: **seeing by wireless**. It was in the quiet, sun-drenched hours of Trinidad, far from any laboratory or workshop, that the theoretical components of mechanical scanning—the Nipkow disc, selenium cells, and light modulation—began to coalesce into a practical obsession in his mind. The failure of the banana farm and the isolation of the tropics led to a profound intellectual conclusion: his life's work was not in growing food, but in growing images.

2.5 Return to Britain and the Initial Shift in Focus towards Wireless Technology.

Baird's self-imposed tropical exile, while medically necessary and intellectually restorative, was ultimately unsustainable. The agricultural venture yielded minimal returns, and his yearning for the intellectual challenge of invention could not be satisfied by managing banana plants. By late 1920, the confluence of financial failure and the deep-seated urge to return to the world of science propelled him back across the Atlantic. He left Trinidad, not cured, but significantly stabilized and with a renewed, fierce focus on a singular goal. His destination was not the harsh industrial landscape of Glasgow, but the relatively mild, seaside town of Bognor Regis on the south coast of England, later moving a short distance to the even more conducive environment of Hastings. This move was a deliberate choice of location—a place where his health could be maintained and where he could dedicate himself entirely to his great idea.

Upon his return, Baird finally acknowledged the inescapable truth of his professional identity: he was an inventor, and his future lay in the most challenging area of electrical communication. All the previous commercial diversions—the jam, the socks, the tropical fruit—were now viewed as necessary, if clumsy, detours taken only because of his health and financial needs. Now, with a measure of physical stability, he determined that he must sink every remaining ounce of energy and capital into the pursuit of **television**. This was the pivotal moment where the scattered energies of the eccentric entrepreneur converged into the singular, relentless focus of the pioneer.

The transition back to invention was marked by a period of intense study and resource gathering. He liquidated any remaining assets and began living on a subsistence budget, prioritizing the purchase of necessary scientific components over personal comforts. The challenge of 'seeing by wireless' had been well-defined by scientists for decades, but the consensus was that it was impossible with the technology of the early 1920s. The prevailing scientific wisdom held that the necessary bandwidth for electronic transmission was impossibly vast, and the creation of a light-sensitive cell rapid enough to capture moving images was years away.

This skepticism, however, only fueled Baird's determination. Drawing directly on his dual education—the mechanical precision learned at Albion Motor Cars and the electrical theory from Glasgow Technical College—he decided to circumvent the daunting electronic problems entirely by focusing on the **mechanical solution**. His approach was characterized by audacious simplicity and pragmatism: he would not wait for advanced electronic components to be developed; he would build a machine using existing, readily available parts. The core components were cheap and accessible: a rudimentary **Nipkow disc** (a spinning cardboard or metal disc perforated with a spiral of holes), a simple light source, and **selenium cells** to convert light into an electrical signal.

This shift marked the true beginning of the television story. Baird took a dusty, academic concept—mechanical scanning—and applied a relentless, practical engineering methodology to it. He was moving from an era of commercial diversion back to his original inventive identity, armed now with the experience of failure and the knowledge that only radical, ground-breaking success could justify his existence and provide the financial freedom his poor health required. The isolation of his new seaside residence became his first laboratory, a place where scraps of metal, lengths of wire, and bits of cardboard were about to be assembled into the foundation of a revolutionary new medium.

Chapter 3: The Theoretical Foundation of Vision (1922–1924)

3.1 The Concept of Image Scanning: Precursors and Theorical Models.

The theoretical concept of television, or "seeing at a distance," was not a novel idea in the early 1920s; it was, in fact, an old, almost mythological problem within physics and electrical engineering circles. The fundamental challenge was universally understood, yet the practical means of overcoming it remained elusive, leading many major corporations and professional scientists to dismiss the endeavor as technologically impossible for the foreseeable future. The crux of the difficulty lay in the difference between transmitting sound and transmitting sight. A sound wave is a serial process; it can be translated into a single, fluctuating electrical signal and sent along a wire or via radio waves. Sight, however, is a parallel process: the eye perceives millions of individual light points simultaneously. To transmit this information electrically, the image had to be broken down, or **serialized**, into a sequence of individual electrical impulses that could be sent one after the other, and then reassembled at the receiving end so quickly that the human eye perceived the whole image at once.

The history of this serialization began decades before Baird. As far back as the 1840s, Alexander Bain had devised a method for transmitting images across telegraph wires using an electro-mechanical scanning process, resulting in the early **facsimile machine**. This was followed by the work of Giovanni Caselli in the 1860s. Their systems proved that an image could be translated into electrical impulses. However, these were static, still images, transmitted over long periods. The challenge of **moving images**—television—required scanning and transmission speeds thousands of times faster. The vital discovery that provided the theoretical bedrock for all practical television systems, both mechanical and later electronic, was the discovery of the element **selenium** in 1873. It was found that selenium's electrical resistance changed proportionally to the intensity of the light falling upon it. This photochemical property provided the necessary transducer, the "electric eye," capable of converting light into a measurable electrical signal.

The most crucial theoretical model that Baird adopted was the **Nipkow disc**, patented in Germany by Paul Nipkow in 1884. Nipkow, a twenty-three-year-old technician, conceived of a flat rotating disc perforated with a spiral of small holes. As the disc spun, each hole traced a path across the object being scanned. When light passed through the holes and struck a selenium cell, the cell registered the light intensity point-by-point, effectively converting the two-dimensional image into a single, rapid, time-varying electrical signal. This was the elegant mechanical solution to the serialization problem. While Nipkow's patent expired years before Baird began his work and he never built a functional model, his conceptual design was the blueprint. Baird's unique contribution was not the invention of the scanning principle itself, but the sheer, indefatigable effort of translating Nipkow's theoretical model into a viable, working physical reality using the imperfect, low-sensitivity components of the 1920s. This required an immense effort in amplification, synchronization, and mechanical tolerance, tasks that others deemed insurmountable. Baird was not pioneering theory, but pioneering application, taking an old diagram and making it run.

3.2 Setting up the First Laboratory in Hastings and the Lack of Funding.

Having returned from the commercial and climatic failure of Trinidad, Baird understood two things: his health demanded a gentle, non-industrial climate, and his mission required total, uninterrupted focus. He chose Hastings, a quiet, southern English coastal town, specifically seeking lodgings that offered both cheap rent and a sympathetic landlady, which was often more crucial than the actual facilities. He found a small, unimposing attic room at 21 Linton Crescent which he immediately converted into his first dedicated television laboratory. This was no high-tech facility; it was a testament to inventive desperation. The lab was cramped, often cold, and lacked all the modern conveniences of a professional research institute.

The crucial constraint shaping this entire phase of his work was the almost absolute lack of funding. Baird was living on the financial scraps remaining from his failed commercial ventures, supplementing his meager income by performing odd electrical repair jobs for local residents. This financial starvation dictated his methodology: he could not afford to buy bespoke, high-precision components or powerful light sources. He was forced into an intense reliance on salvage, adaptation, and sheer mechanical ingenuity—the very traits honed during his early boyhood experiments in Helensburgh. This era of his life is often romanticized, but it was a period of genuine struggle, marked by poor nutrition, constant financial anxiety, and the persistent dampness of the English coast which challenged his precarious health.

The lack of funds meant that every piece of apparatus had to serve multiple purposes. Electric motors were sourced from discarded fans or phonographs. The core optical elements, the Nipkow discs, had to be fashioned crudely from scrap metal or, more commonly, thick cardboard, often cut with a kitchen knife and held together with glue. The essential photoreceptors, the selenium cells, which were themselves extremely slow and insensitive by modern standards, had to be meticulously wired and constantly adjusted. The challenge was not just making the parts work, but making these very low-quality parts work together with enough synchronization and speed to create a barely discernible image. His scientific pursuit was conducted in a state of profound material poverty, a reality that forced him to become the ultimate master of improvisation.

His neighbors and landlady were naturally perplexed by the erratic behavior emanating from his attic laboratory—the whirring, clicking, and scraping noises of the primitive motors, the flickering arc lights, and the frequent smell of burnt insulation. The inventor was perceived as a strange eccentric, pouring his life into a crazy experiment in an age when radio was still considered the height of technology. This isolation from the mainstream scientific community was both a curse and a blessing. It meant he was starved of resources and collaborative intellectual feedback, but it also freed him from the prevailing, dismissive dogma of established engineers who believed the electronic solution was the only path forward. Baird's conviction, born of personal desperation and a lifetime of mechanical tinkering, was that a mechanical solution was possible now, not years in the future, and he was determined to prove it using his tea chest and his last shillings.

3.3 The Role of the Nipkow Disc and the Principles of Mechanical Scanning.

Baird's mechanical system was an outright defiance of the emerging electronic age, a glorious, sputtering triumph of clockwork mechanics over the theoretical limitations of vacuum tubes. The entire system pivoted on the elegant simplicity of the **Nipkow disc**. Understanding the disc's role is essential to appreciating the nature of Baird's first successes. The disc itself was an ingenious solution to the problem of **spatial to temporal conversion**. A television image contains hundreds, or even thousands, of individual points of light and shadow, all existing simultaneously. The Nipkow disc provided the means to process these points sequentially, one by one.

The principle is straightforward: the disc is cut with a series of small, uniform holes arranged in a tight spiral. The number of holes corresponds to the number of horizontal scanning lines in the resulting image. For Baird's earliest successful demonstrations, this was a meager **30-line resolution**, meaning 30 holes spiraled around the disc. The subject to be televised—say, a doll or a person—was brightly illuminated. As the disc spun rapidly, the first hole in the spiral passed across the top of the subject, admitting light to a photo-sensitive cell behind the disc. As the disc continued to rotate, the second hole, slightly lower than the first, traced an adjacent path, and so on, until the thirtieth hole completed the full scan across the bottom of the image area.

In a fraction of a second, the entire scene was converted into a single stream of variable electrical energy: a bright point of light hitting the cell generated a high electrical current; a dark point generated a low current. This electrical waveform—the video signal—was then amplified and sent via wire or radio. At the receiver, an identical, synchronized disc spun at the same speed. Instead of a selenium cell, the receiving disc had a **neon lamp** positioned behind it. The incoming electrical signal was fed to the neon lamp, causing its brightness to flicker in precise synchronization with the signal. When the high signal arrived (from a bright part of the image), the lamp glowed brightly. When the low signal arrived (from a dark part), it dimmed.

The genius of the mechanical system was the perfect correspondence between the transmitter and the receiver. As the first hole passed over the first line of the image at the transmitter, the corresponding first hole on the receiver's disc was passing in front of the neon lamp. Because the light from the lamp was being flashed in sequence with the electrical signal, the tiny, momentary pinprick of light reconstructed the brightness of that specific point of the original image. The speed of rotation was crucial: for the eye to perceive a moving, continuous image, the entire process had to happen fast enough to exploit the **persistence of vision**—the physiological fact that the human eye retains an image for a split second after it vanishes. Baird's 30-line system ran at 12.5 frames per second. The Nipkow disc, therefore, was not merely a mechanical component; it was the physical clockwork engine of serialization, the translator that turned light into time and then back into light, a concept that captivated Baird and offered a pathway to an immediate, though low-resolution, solution.

3.4 Initial Apparatus: Scraps, Sealing Wax, and the Tea Chest.

The physical construction of Baird's first successful apparatus in his cramped Hastings attic is one of the most famous and compelling anecdotes in the history of invention. It represents the quintessential image of the lone, resourceful genius battling insurmountable odds with nothing more than junk and sheer willpower. The equipment was less a refined machine and more an assemblage of domestic debris and scavenged components, a visible manifestation of his chronic lack of funds and his engineer's resourcefulness. The enduring image of this primitive apparatus, often cited in engineering textbooks, is the **tea chest** that formed the structural base of the transmitter. This wooden box, salvaged perhaps from a local grocer, provided the frame upon which the entire nascent television system was mounted, giving the equipment a haphazard, almost absurd appearance that belied the complexity of the task it performed.

The crucial Nipkow discs themselves were initially made from thick **cardboard**, sourced from hats or packaging, cut and punctured with holes, and sometimes reinforced with glue and string. The spinning mechanism was powered by small electric motors, often salvaged from domestic appliances or toys, whose speed had to be laboriously regulated. This was a critical point of difficulty: the synchronization between the transmitter and receiver discs was paramount. A slight variation in speed would result in a warped or unrecognizable image at the receiving end, an effect called **synchronization drift**. Baird's early solutions for this were purely mechanical and often involved delicate, manual adjustments. The holes in the discs, the alignment of the lenses, and the mounting of the entire mechanism were held in place not by precision screws and machined brackets, but by common materials like **sealing wax** and glue. This use of sealing wax, usually reserved for formal documents, became a metaphor for his entire enterprise: a low-tech, almost desperate binder holding together a high-concept invention.

The photoreceptor was a selenium cell. Because selenium cells of the era were notoriously insensitive, the subject had to be illuminated with blinding intensity. Baird used **arc lamps**, powerful sources of light that also generated tremendous heat and noise, turning his small attic lab into a frequently uncomfortable and slightly hazardous environment. The light reflected from the subject passed through the rotating holes of the cardboard disc and struck the cell, generating the minuscule electrical signal. This signal then had to pass through a bank of bulky **thermionic valves**—early vacuum tube amplifiers—to be strong enough for transmission. These valves, though essential, were themselves noisy, unreliable, and consumed a lot of power, adding to the instability of the system.

Anecdotes from this period confirm the inventor's almost manic dedication. One famous account describes how the vibration of the crude apparatus was so violent that the tea chest would often shake itself apart, requiring immediate and patient reassembly. Another tells of his near electrocution when working with the high voltages required for the arc lamps, a constant hazard of his poorly insulated, hand-built laboratory. The apparatus, with its darning needles serving as axles, its bicycle lenses focused crudely, and its main structural support being a wooden box, was a marvel of resourcefulness. It proved that the essence of invention is not expensive components, but the radical recombination of existing, mundane materials to solve a novel, profound problem. The tea chest television was less about beautiful engineering and more about the dogged, undeniable proof of concept.

3.5 The Vision: Transmitting a Moving Image, not just Static Pictures.

The distinction between transmitting a static image and transmitting a moving image was the conceptual chasm that separated facsimile technology from true television, and it was the bridge Baird was singularly determined to build. For decades, engineers had successfully transmitted still photographs and documents point-by-point, a process that could take several minutes. Baird's ambition was far greater: he sought to transmit life, movement, and instantaneous change. The key to this vision lay in the physiological limitation of the human eye, known as **persistence of vision**. The human retina and brain retain an image for approximately one-sixteenth of a second after the image source is removed. To create the illusion of continuous motion, a sequence of individual, slightly varied still images—**frames**—must be presented to the eye faster than the persistence time. The standard required for smooth, flickering-free motion was determined to be around ten to sixteen frames per second.

Baird focused his entire mechanical system—the speed of the motors, the number of lines, the precision of the synchronization—on achieving this required frame rate. His 30-line system was designed to rotate the disc 12.5 times per second, translating into 12.5 complete image scans, or frames, per second. The success of this rate meant that when the signal was received and illuminated the neon lamp behind the receiving Nipkow disc, the resulting flickering points of light blended together in the viewer's eye. Instead of seeing a rapid sequence of discrete scans, the viewer perceived a continuous, coherent image.

This focus on the moving image was critical to Baird's identity as a true pioneer. He was not just refining an existing technology; he was creating a new medium. While other researchers were content with demonstrating the theoretical possibility of photoelectric transmission or achieving high-resolution still image transfer, Baird was intent on delivering the illusion of life. This ambitious goal introduced immense technical difficulty. The higher the resolution (the more lines of scanning), the more detail could be captured, but this required an even faster scanning speed, which in turn demanded a prohibitively large **bandwidth**—the electrical capacity needed to carry the signal. Baird's decision to use a minimal **30-line** resolution was a masterstroke of pragmatic trade-off. It sacrificed detail for speed. The resulting image was crude—a reddish, flickering, blurry outline—but it possessed the one quality that mattered: **movement**.

The importance of this realization—that a low-definition moving image was a greater psychological and technological breakthrough than a high-definition static one—cannot be overstated. It was the moment vision became television. It meant that a story could be told, an event could be witnessed, and the medium itself was born. Baird's perseverance through the countless, frustrating failures of his initial contraptions was fueled by this vision: he did not merely want to send a pattern of light and dark; he wanted to transmit the essence of performance, communication, and visual narrative. The technical challenge was fierce, but the ultimate prize, the ability to transmit a human face that could wink or smile, drove him forward through the darkest hours of his financial and physical struggles in the quiet seaside attic of Hastings.

Chapter 4: The First Breakthrough (1924–1926)

4.1 The First Successful Transmission of an Outline Image (The Maltese Cross).

By early 1924, John Logie Baird had moved his improvised laboratory from the quiet isolation of Hastings to a slightly larger, though still cramped and chaotic, space at 22 Frith Street in the heart of Soho, London. This move was strategic, driven not by technical necessity but by commercial imperative: he needed to be near the pulse of the nation's financial and media capital to attract attention and, more importantly, investors. Despite the superior resources theoretically available in London, the core apparatus remained a cobbled-together marvel of ingenuity and desperation, held together by sealing wax, scrap wood, and wire. His daily life was still a hand-to-mouth existence, but the focus was absolute.

His relentless tinkering paid off in a crucial, defining moment in February 1924. After innumerable failures, frustrating synchronization drifts, and the constant blowing of fuses, Baird achieved the **first truly successful transmission of an outline image** that was coherent and stable enough to be definitively recognized by an independent observer. The subject of this historic transmission was a simple, unambiguous pattern: a **Maltese Cross**. This wasn't just a flickering shadow; it was a dark, distinct shape projected onto a light background.

The reason for choosing the Maltese Cross was entirely pragmatic. Given the extremely low resolution of his 30-line scanning system and the poor sensitivity of the selenium cells, the image was fundamentally limited to conveying high-contrast, simple shapes. A human face or a complex photograph would have blurred into an unrecognizable mass of light and shadow. The cross, with its sharp, defined edges and high contrast, was the perfect test subject. The transmitter, using the spinning cardboard Nipkow disc, scanned the cross, converting its silhouette into a strong, variable electrical signal. The receiver, synchronized to the transmitter, reassembled this signal, and observers could clearly discern the distinct four-pointed shape on the screen of the neon lamp.

This breakthrough was enormously significant. It transcended the theoretical possibility of image transmission and provided tangible proof that Baird's specific mechanical system, however crude, was fundamentally viable. It demonstrated that the synchronization of the discs worked well enough, and the amplifying circuits were sufficient to transmit a recognizable visual pattern across a short distance via wires. Though it was only an outline, it was a visual representation transmitted, not merely a sound converted into light, marking the moment that **television moved from a dream to a demonstrated reality**. The success with the Maltese Cross fueled Baird's confidence and was the necessary initial evidence he needed to present to the skeptical financial world, initiating the shift from isolated attic inventor to public showman of science.

4.2 Media Attention and the Move to Soho, London, to Find Investors.

The successful, stable transmission of the Maltese Cross outline was a turning point, not only technically but strategically. Baird was acutely aware that scientific achievement alone, especially one conducted with such humble materials, would not bring him the substantial capital needed to develop the system further. His immediate priority became publicity and finance. The move to Soho, initiated earlier, now proved its worth. Frith Street was close to Fleet Street, the hub of the British press, and the city's financial institutions.

Baird, a naturally reserved and often ailing man, transformed himself into an energetic, if still slightly eccentric, promoter. He began actively contacting local newspapers and journals, inviting reporters to his dingy upper-floor laboratory to witness the miracle of the moving shadows. The initial press reaction was mixed. Some journalists were genuinely awestruck by the sheer novelty of the demonstration, recognizing the profound implications of seeing by wireless. Others, however, were deeply skeptical, regarding the noisy, flickering, sealing-wax-and-scrap-metal apparatus as the work of a charlatan or a deluded enthusiast. The fact that the image was so blurry and reddish, and the apparatus so visually crude, often undermined the credibility of the invention in the eyes of the less imaginative observer.

One particularly famous encounter involved a visit to the offices of the **Daily Express** newspaper. A reporter was sent to investigate the persistent reports of the "vision at a distance" inventor. Upon hearing the description of the inventor—a gaunt, sickly looking man who claimed to be transmitting faces through the air using motors and cardboard discs—the news editor was seized by alarm. He immediately instructed his staff to get rid of the "lunatic" before he could cause trouble, fearing that Baird was a crank who might pose a physical danger. This anecdote perfectly illustrates the gap between Baird's radical vision and the average person's comprehension of the technology at the time.

Despite the initial resistance, enough positive reports surfaced to attract a small circle of interested individuals, primarily businessmen and investors willing to take a high-risk gamble on a seemingly impossible technology. They were less concerned with the scientific purism of the system and more with its immense commercial potential. This growing interest led to the formation of the first financial vehicles dedicated to Baird's work. It was not the large-scale corporate backing he craved, but the necessary seed money that allowed him to secure better components, hire a single assistant, and continue his experiments without the constant threat of eviction or starvation. The publicity—even the skeptical variety—was successful in achieving its primary goal: elevating the "Televisor" from a private hobby to a public phenomenon that demanded serious consideration.

4.3 The Critical Day: January 26, 1926 – The Public Demonstration to the Royal Institution.

The success with simple outlines proved the concept, but the true validation Baird sought was from the scientific establishment itself, a community that had largely dismissed mechanical television as a dead end. This critical validation arrived on **January 26, 1926**, a date now enshrined as a milestone in the history of communication. On this day, Baird formally demonstrated his working system to members of the **Royal Institution of Great Britain**, one of the world's most prestigious and conservative scientific bodies, along with a number of reporters and fellow scientists.

The demonstration took place in his Soho laboratory, presenting an almost comical juxtaposition: serious, frock-coated academics gathered in the inventor's messy, tiny workshop, surrounded by humming motors and flickering lights. Baird was keenly aware that this audience would not be satisfied with the transmission of a mere Maltese Cross; they demanded proof that the system could handle a human subject. For this demonstration, he had prepared a significantly improved version of his apparatus, though it remained mechanically based and still operated at the original **30-line resolution** and **12.5 frames per second**.

The importance of this demonstration lay in its **witnesses** and their subsequent affidavits. A representative group, including Professor Edward Fournier d'Albe, confirmed that they were able to clearly observe images that conveyed not just light and shade, but the **gradations of tone** necessary to depict a recognizable, living person. The system was now capable of true **half-tones**, not just silhouettes. The fact that this achievement was witnessed and documented by independent scientific authorities, not just sensationalist journalists, was revolutionary. It removed the technology from the realm of quackery and planted it firmly in the world of proven physical science.

This event secured Baird his place as a pioneer. Prior to this, many believed that only an electronic system, years in the future, could overcome the technical hurdles of bandwidth and sensitivity. Baird demonstrated that a simple, mechanical approach, utilizing existing 1920s technology, could transmit a moving, recognizable image. The official documentation of this event provided the credibility necessary to attract further, more serious investment and to finally initiate the next, crucial phase of development: transforming the laboratory curiosity into a broadcast medium. The Royal Institution demonstration effectively silenced the most vocal skeptics and announced to the world that television was no longer a science fiction fantasy, but an impending reality.

4.4 The Demonstration of 'Televisor': Transmission of a Recognisable Human Face (Siki).

The most challenging aspect of Baird's work was always the transition from transmitting simple geometric shapes to transmitting the most complex and nuanced subject: the human face. A face requires the system to handle subtle variations in light and shadow, the fine detail of eyes and mouth, and the movement of muscles. For the January 1926 demonstration, Baird needed a clear, undeniable demonstration of a recognizable human face, not just an outline. The problem was that even the best arc lamps of the time were not powerful enough to fully illuminate a subject with enough intensity for the notoriously poor selenium cells to register the full range of light.

To overcome the sensitivity issue, Baird initially experimented with **puppets and dummies**, hoping to simulate a face, but the effect lacked the necessary realism. He required a living human subject, but one who was static enough and close enough to the scanning aperture to yield a strong signal. The technical solution he devised was simple: he transmitted a moving image of a person's hand first, then a face. To ensure the face was sufficiently illuminated, he employed extremely powerful light sources, which made the experience intensely uncomfortable for his early test subjects.

The subject of the very first recognizable human face transmitted was not a scientist or a famous figure, but a young office boy named **William Taynton**, who worked in the building below Baird's lab. In one of the most famous incidents of early television history, Taynton refused to stay in position under the glare of the blinding arc lights. Frustrated, Baird ran down the stairs and returned with another young man from the street—a local newspaper delivery boy known as **'Siki'** (though the name Siki is often associated with the test, the identity of the boy remains slightly fluid, Taynton being the most confirmed of the early subjects). Baird bribed the boy with a few shillings to sit in the intense heat and blinding light of the transmitter.

Siki's face was positioned directly against the scanning aperture. As the Nipkow disc spun, the image signal was sent to the receiver in the adjacent room. The resulting image on the neon lamp was tiny, reddish, and flickering, but it was unmistakably the recognizable face of the young boy, complete with the subtle variations of half-tone that defined his features. When Siki moved his head or waved his hand, the image on the receiver moved correspondingly. This was the moment true television—the transmission of a recognizable, moving human subject—was born.

The ability to transmit a recognizable human face was the cultural threshold. It meant that communication could be personal, immediate, and intimate. It was the crucial leap that transformed the mechanical apparatus from a scientific curiosity into a potential social revolution. Baird's **Televisor** had finally achieved what it promised: to bring sight across the wire, making the world immediately smaller and connecting people visually in a way that radio never could.

4.5 Technical Specifications of the First Operational System (30-line resolution).

The operational system publicly demonstrated by John Logie Baird in 1926, which successfully transmitted moving, recognizable human subjects, was a marvel of mechanical engineering constrained by the limitations of 1920s electrical technology. To understand its revolutionary nature, one must appreciate its key, defining technical specifications, which are minimalist by modern standards but were monumental achievements at the time.

The most defining characteristic was the **30-line resolution**. This number refers to the number of horizontal lines into which the image was broken down during the scanning process. This was a deliberate and pragmatic choice. The lower the line count, the less detail the image contained, but critically, the less **bandwidth** was required to transmit the signal. A high-resolution image would have required electronic components and radio transmission capacity that simply did not exist. By choosing 30 lines, Baird kept the data rate manageable for existing wireless and wire technologies. In comparison, modern broadcast television uses resolutions of 525 to over 1000 lines. The 30-line image was tiny (often only a few inches high) and very crude, but it was demonstrably a moving picture.

The **frame rate** was set at **12.5 frames per second**. As discussed, this rate was the minimum required to exploit the **persistence of vision** and create the illusion of smooth motion, though the image still suffered from noticeable flicker. To achieve this, the Nipkow discs—both the transmitter and the receiver discs—had to be rotated at a synchronized speed of **750 revolutions per minute (RPM)**. Maintaining this precise synchronization using simple, non-electronic motors and governors was one of Baird's greatest technical hurdles, often solved with mechanical braking systems and subtle manual adjustments.

The essential components were:

1. **Transmitter Disc:** A large, often cardboard or metal disc with 30 holes arranged in a spiral pattern. It was spun by an electric motor.
2. **Photoreceptor:** A highly sensitive, but slow, **selenium cell**. Its sluggish response time contributed to the blurring in the moving image, but it was the best available light-to-electricity converter. The subject had to be illuminated by extremely bright **arc lamps** due to the selenium cell's low sensitivity.
3. **Amplification:** The extremely weak electrical signal generated by the selenium cell had to be greatly boosted by a series of noisy, power-hungry **thermionic valve amplifiers** before it was strong enough to be transmitted.
4. **Receiver Disc:** An identical 30-hole Nipkow disc, synchronized to the transmitter.
5. **Display:** A small, low-pressure **neon lamp**. The video signal was fed directly to the lamp, causing its brightness to fluctuate rapidly. The light flickering through the holes of the spinning receiver disc recreated the image point-by-point.

This system was inherently **mechanical** and fundamentally **low-definition**. Its great triumph was not its technical elegance but its **immediacy**. It was the first **operational, demonstrable** system of true television, proving that the basic principles of image scanning and reconstruction were correct, and paving the way for the massive technological leap that would follow in the subsequent decade.

Chapter 5: Commercialisation and Public Exposure (1926–1928)

5.1 Formation of the Baird Television Development Company (BTDC).

Following the critical public demonstration to the Royal Institution in January 1926, the era of the tea-chest television was decisively over. The moment the scientific community acknowledged that Baird had achieved the impossible—the stable transmission of a recognizable, moving human face—the invention moved from the realm of eccentric hobby to a commercially viable proposition. The validation gave Baird the necessary leverage to secure the substantial financial backing required to transition his messy Soho lab into a corporate entity. This critical step was the formation of the **Baird Television Development Company** or BTDC, in April 1927. The company's immediate purpose was to capitalize on the patents Baird had painstakingly secured and to secure a monopoly on the commercial exploitation of mechanical television.

The formation involved a familiar clash between the inventor's desire for pure technical development and the financiers' demand for immediate commercial return. Baird, chronically frail and socially awkward, was fundamentally unsuited to the cutthroat world of corporate finance, but he was forced to navigate it to realize his dream. He was provided with working capital, but control of the company was necessarily ceded to the investors and businessmen who had recognized the enormous potential in his invention. Figures like Major A. G. Church and Captain O. G. S. Bailey, men with connections to politics, finance, and the military, were brought in to manage the corporate structure and strategy. Baird's title was effectively that of Chief Inventor, focusing his efforts on technical development while the Board focused on licensing and marketing.

The initial capitalization, while significant compared to the few shillings Baird had been scraping by on previously, was still modest relative to the vast research budgets of competitors like General Electric or Westinghouse in the United States. This relative underfunding would become a chronic problem, forcing the BTDC to focus on rapid commercialization of the existing, low-definition system rather than investing in long-term, high-definition electronic research that was quietly being developed by others. The company's immediate goal was twofold: first, to manufacture and sell the **Televisor**, the domestic receiving apparatus, to a growing market of radio enthusiasts, and second, to persuade the government and the British Broadcasting Corporation, the BBC, to grant official wavelengths for television broadcasting.

The establishment of the BTDC marked a profound psychological shift for Baird. He was no longer the lone, struggling inventor, but the figurehead of a pioneering industry. The company allowed him to hire a small team of engineers and assistants, moving the entire operation from the cramped Frith Street attic to larger, more suitable premises. This provided him with the necessary resources to refine his apparatus, replacing the cardboard discs and sealing wax with machined metal parts, more efficient motors, and specially constructed amplifiers. However, the pressure intensified. He was now accountable to shareholders, and every technical setback was a financial liability, transforming the joy of pure experimentation into the stressful necessity of scheduled product delivery. His personal success was now inextricably linked to the volatile fortunes of the company he helped create.

5.2 The Importance of Shortwave Radio and the First Experiments with Broadcast.

With the formation of the BTDC, the challenge shifted from transmitting an image across a room via wires to broadcasting it wirelessly across entire cities, a monumental leap that hinged entirely on the efficient use of the radio spectrum. The underlying issue was **bandwidth**. A 30-line television signal, flickering at 12.5 frames per second, required a much wider range of frequencies—a much larger bandwidth—than a simple audio broadcast. This requirement immediately complicated the relationship with the broadcasting authorities.

In the 1920s, the medium wave frequencies, which offered reliable long-distance coverage and were suitable for standard amplitude modulation (AM) radio, were already saturated with sound broadcasts. The BBC and the Post Office, which controlled all radio licenses, were deeply reluctant to allocate large chunks of this valuable spectrum to an unproven, low-definition visual medium. Baird's mechanical system, while requiring less bandwidth than the high-definition electronic systems that would follow, still demanded a spectrum slice wide enough to carry the necessary video information.

To overcome this, Baird and his team pioneered the use of the **shortwave** bands, or what we now call high frequency (HF) and later very high frequency (VHF). While these bands presented propagation challenges, they were far less crowded and allowed for the wider bandwidth necessary for video signals. Baird began conducting experimental broadcasts from his own facilities, often without official sanction, which put him in constant friction with the Post Office regulators. The earliest solution was ingenious but cumbersome for the viewer: the vision signal was transmitted on one wavelength, while the accompanying sound was transmitted on a completely different, standard BBC medium wave frequency.

The viewer attempting to receive these broadcasts at home had to tune two separate radio receivers simultaneously, a complex act of coordination that resulted in frequent synchronization errors. If the vision receiver drifted slightly out of sync, the image would tear or become scrambled. Despite these difficulties, these initial experimental transmissions, conducted as early as 1926 and ramping up significantly by 1928, marked the true beginning of public television broadcasting. They were raw, irregular, and often transmitted late at night when the medium wave band was clearer, but they proved that the signal could be sent wirelessly over a considerable distance.

These experiments were not just technical exercises; they were political statements. By demonstrating that television could, in fact, be broadcast using the available technology and a practical frequency band, Baird put immense pressure on the BBC and the government to formally recognize and incorporate television into the national broadcasting structure. His use of shortwave proved that the mechanical system was viable for mass communication, setting the stage for the formal trials that would define the next decade of British television.

5.3 Development of the Phonovision System (Recording Television).

The problem of how to record and archive television images was almost as challenging as the problem of transmission itself. The fleeting, low-resolution visual signal existed only for the moment it was scanned and displayed. Film was an option, but cumbersome. Baird's solution was a typically pragmatic, mechanical approach that bypassed the need for high-speed film and instead utilized an existing, widespread technology: the **gramophone record**. He called this system **Phonovision**, a term which perfectly encapsulated its function—recording vision onto phonograph grooves.

The technical basis for Phonovision was the inherent nature of the 30-line signal. Because the mechanical scanner broke the image down into a single stream of light variations, and these variations were translated into electrical currents that fluctuated in the audio frequency range, the entire video signal could be treated essentially as a complex sound. By feeding this video signal into a standard recording lathe, the resulting waveform could be physically etched into the shellac of a conventional 78 RPM gramophone record. The varying depth and lateral movement of the groove corresponded to the varying light and shade of the televised image.

The revolutionary aspect of Phonovision was that it offered the world's first successful method of **time-shifted viewing and archiving** visual content. Although the original intent was a commercial product, its enduring legacy lies in the fact that these records are the oldest surviving artifacts of televised images, predating magnetic tape and modern digital media by decades. The records captured broadcasts from 1927 onward, preserving the ghostly, flickering images of early test subjects and actors.

However, the fidelity of the system was extremely poor. The Phonovision discs suffered from multiple layers of degradation. First, the 30-line original image was already crude. Second, the records themselves introduced immense **noise** and **distortion** due to the physical limitations of the groove cutting and playback process, reducing the quality even further. The synchronization of the playback motor was also highly sensitive; any slight variation in the record player's speed would completely scramble the already faint image. Enthusiasts attempting to play Phonovision records required a specially modified Televisor receiver and an incredibly stable turntable motor, making playback a highly technical challenge.

Despite its commercial failure as a mass-market product—the image quality was simply too low and the playback too difficult for the general public—Phonovision demonstrated Baird's relentless drive to solve every aspect of the television problem, from capture to transmission to storage. It stands as a technological curiosity, a perfectly logical, yet ultimately limiting, mechanical answer to a problem that would later be solved more elegantly by electronics. The existence of these records today provides a priceless, direct window into the dawn of the moving image broadcast, a testament to the fact that Baird succeeded in capturing time on a shellac disc.

5.4 Public Demonstrations at Selfridges and Other Major Department Stores.

To raise capital and public awareness, the BTDC needed to present television not just as a laboratory curiosity, but as a practical, commercially available home appliance. The company's marketing strategy revolved around a series of spectacular and highly publicized public demonstrations, often staged in the most visible commercial venues. The most famous and influential of these was the exhibition held at **Selfridges** department store in London's Oxford Street, a venue renowned for showcasing the latest technology and luxury goods.

Starting in 1925, and continuing with greater frequency after the company's formation, these department store demonstrations were crucial for establishing the concept of the Televisor in the public mind. The spectacle was designed to draw crowds: the transmitter was set up in a back room, and the receiving apparatus was placed prominently in a window or on the main floor. Crowds would gather, watching with a mixture of awe and confusion as a reddish, flickering image of a person, often an assistant, or sometimes a puppet, materialized on the small screen.

The demonstrations, while visually impressive for the time, were technologically challenging. The images were small—typically no more than two or three inches square—and constantly required fine-tuning. The public was shown clear movement and rough facial features, proving the magic was real, but the low quality ensured that television was initially perceived as a novelty item for wealthy enthusiasts rather than an essential medium. However, the psychological impact was immense. For the first time, people saw that the future promised by radio—the transmission of visual information—had arrived. This immediacy generated feverish excitement in the press, further fueling investment and commercial demand.

The commercial objective was to sell the **Televisor kit**, which consisted of the mechanical receiver, the neon lamp, and the necessary valves and motor controls, designed to connect to an existing radio set. These kits were initially expensive and complex to assemble and operate, appealing primarily to technically minded radio amateurs who relished the challenge of building and calibrating the device. The sales generated, though small in number, provided the necessary cash flow for the BTDC.

These public exhibitions served as a vital bridge between the secluded lab and the living room. Baird understood that the public could forgive low resolution if the apparatus was available and demonstrable. The constant exposure in places like Selfridges created cultural momentum, forcing the national broadcaster and government to take notice. The demonstrations proved the existence of a commercial market, however small, for the apparatus, solidifying Baird's position as the inventor who successfully brought the visual medium out of theoretical physics and into the nascent consumer electronics market. They were a brilliant piece of commercial theatre, cementing television's place as the next great technological sensation.

5.5 Growing Media Rivalry and Skepticism from the Scientific Establishment.

The widespread media attention and successful public demonstrations that propelled Baird's company were a double-edged sword. While they generated necessary capital and public excitement, they also provoked intense **rivalry and skepticism** from two powerful camps: established media corporations and the academic scientific community.

Major corporations, particularly those involved in wireless and electrical manufacturing, viewed Baird's mechanical system with deep suspicion. Companies like **Marconi** and later the combined **EMI-Marconi** considered mechanical scanning to be a technological cul-de-sac. Their in-house engineers and scientists were already focused on the theoretical potential of the **cathode ray tube** (CRT) systems, the purely electronic approach pioneered by individuals like Vladimir Zworykin and Philo Farnsworth in the United States. These electronic systems, while requiring decades to perfect, promised the potential for vastly higher resolution (hundreds of lines) and brighter, more stable pictures, entirely devoid of the noise and flicker inherent in a mechanical disc spinning at high speed.

To these rivals, Baird was a brilliant but fundamentally misdirected amateur, whose low-definition, flickering image was an embarrassing distraction from the true path of electronic television. This corporate skepticism manifested as subtle but persistent media criticism, often emphasizing the crudeness of the 30-line picture and pointing out the system's physical limitations, such as the impossibility of making the receiving screen much larger than a few inches without an unwieldy apparatus.

The scientific establishment, which had begrudgingly acknowledged the technical success of the 1926 demonstration, also remained wary. Academic critics questioned the scalability of the Nipkow disc. To achieve higher definition—say, 100 or 200 lines—the disc would have to spin exponentially faster, creating immense mechanical and synchronization problems that seemed insurmountable. The required bandwidth would also explode, making broadcast on existing infrastructure impossible. Baird's focus on mechanical innovation was seen as a resistance to the fundamental move towards purely electronic physics.

This intense rivalry placed Baird in a paradoxical and difficult position. He possessed the world's only *working* television system, one that could be demonstrated and sold *today*, whereas his rivals had only promises of a technologically superior system *tomorrow*. He became the champion of the available technology, which meant he was constantly fighting the future. This dynamic forced the BTDC to invest heavily in publicity and rapid commercialization, further stretching resources that should have been dedicated to long-term research into high-definition. Baird was trapped, having to defend his pioneering practicality against the theoretical elegance of electronic potential, a battle that would define the rest of his career and ultimately lead to the end of the mechanical television era.

Chapter 6: The Dawn of Global Television (1928-1929)

6.1 The Historic Transatlantic Transmission from London to New York.

The achievement of successfully demonstrating television in a laboratory setting was immense, but the true prize, both technically and culturally, was conquering the vast expanse of the Atlantic Ocean. For wireless enthusiasts, the transatlantic transmission of any signal was the ultimate benchmark of technological mastery, and for John Logie Baird, it represented the opportunity to silence the critics who insisted that his low-definition signal was too fragile and bandwidth-hungry to survive long-distance transmission. On February 9, 1928, Baird realized this monumental ambition, sending the first live television images from his transmitter in **Coulsdon, Surrey, England, to a receiver located in Hartsdale, New York, USA.**

This historic feat was not a seamless, instantaneous broadcast like those we know today; it was a complex operation relying on shortwave radio's unique propagation characteristics. The signal, transmitted using the call sign G2TV, had to be carefully timed to exploit the ionospheric layer's ability to reflect shortwave frequencies back to Earth, known as "skip." This meant the broadcast had to be conducted at specific times when atmospheric conditions were optimal for spanning the thousands of miles. The receiving station was set up in the laboratory of Benjamin J. Clapp, one of Baird's enthusiastic American partners. The image received was, predictably, faint and flickering—a crude, orange-red silhouette on a two-inch screen—but the recognizable outline of a human face was undeniably transmitted across continents.

The subject of the broadcast was a small toy doll, followed by the face of Baird's assistant, **Vicars Foote**. The message was simple: "Hello," accompanied by a nod of the head. Yet, the impact was profound. The world's press hailed it as a technological miracle, comparing it to Marconi's initial transatlantic radio signal. Baird had not merely demonstrated the technical feasibility of television; he had established its potential as a global medium, shattering the limitations of localized broadcasting. This accomplishment was a massive strategic victory for the **Baird Television Development Company (BTDC)**, providing invaluable international publicity and immediately increasing the perceived value of their patents. It also acted as a powerful challenge to his American competitors, who were still largely focused on local wired or short-range transmission systems. Despite the fragile nature of the reception and the inherent crudity of the 30-line image, the event solidified Baird's reputation as the undisputed pioneer of practical television. The world saw that mechanical television worked, and that it could shrink the world.

6.2 The First Outdoor Television Broadcast (The Epsom Derby).

Having conquered the distance with the transatlantic transmission, the next logical challenge for Baird was to prove that television was capable of handling the complexities of outdoor action and movement, moving beyond the static close-up of a face in a dark studio. This was a critical test because critics argued that the low scanning rate of the 30-line system—just 12.5 frames per second—would result in severe blurring and motion artifacts when attempting to capture fast-moving subjects under natural light. Baird selected an event synonymous with speed, excitement, and national interest: **The Epsom Derby** in June 1928.

Broadcasting the Derby was an immense technical undertaking. It required overcoming the challenge of transmitting images captured not in a controlled, artificially lit studio, but under the variable and bright illumination of an outdoor setting. The key innovation for this broadcast was the use of a modified mechanical scanning system, relying on the **Flying Spot Scanner** technique for the camera, which was inherently difficult to deploy outdoors. The camera apparatus, large and highly sensitive to ambient light, was set up close to the racetrack, requiring a complex arrangement of lenses and mirrors to capture the horses as they passed a specific point.

The actual broadcast was experimental and highly irregular. The images that reached the receiving sets—primarily those set up for demonstration purposes in London—were received by a select few. The picture quality was extremely low, with the horses appearing as indistinct, flickering shapes against the backdrop of the rails and crowds. It was, however, indisputably a transmission of moving images captured outside. Crucially, the broadcast proved that the **photoelectric cells** used in the camera were sensitive enough to translate natural daylight and dynamic action into a usable electrical signal.

The significance of the Epsom Derby broadcast lay less in its image quality and more in its demonstration of television's potential application. It showed the media and the public that television was not merely a medium for static studio portraits, but could be used for **live sports coverage and outside events**, the precise content that would eventually drive consumer demand for the medium decades later. It demonstrated the engineering ingenuity of the BTDC team and added further momentum to the push for regular, official broadcasting rights from the BBC, showing that television could capture the excitement and scale of real-world events, even if the result was a shaky, low-definition outline of a racehorse.

6.3 Experiments with Colour Television (The Trichromatic Method).

With monochrome television established as a technical reality, Baird immediately turned his attention to the next frontier: **colour television**. His relentless drive for innovation meant he was never content with the current state of technology. Just as he had solved the transmission problem using mechanical means, he tackled the colour problem by applying the same principles. In July 1928, just a few months after his transatlantic triumph, he unveiled a crude but effective demonstration of the world's first successful colour television system, utilizing what became known as the **Trichromatic Method**.

Baird's system was an additive colour process, based on the principle that any visible colour could be reproduced by combining the three primary colours of light: red, green, and blue. The core of his colour apparatus remained the mechanical Nipkow disc. To achieve colour scanning, he used a system incorporating three spirals of apertures on the disc. These apertures were covered with three different colour filters: a red filter, a green filter, and a blue filter. As the disc spun, the filters sequentially scanned the scene or object being televised.

On the receiver end, the images were displayed using a similar, synchronized disc with corresponding colour filters. As the red filtered aperture scanned the scene, the red filter on the receiver would pass the light from the corresponding image, and so on for green and blue. The eye's persistence of vision—the same phenomenon that makes motion pictures work—blended the rapidly alternating red, green, and blue images into a single, if often unstable, full-colour picture. The demonstration subject was a bowl of flowers, chosen specifically for its vibrant range of colours.

While a genuine breakthrough, the images were even more rudimentary than their monochrome counterparts. The colour registration was poor, the images flickered intensely due to the low scan rate, and the entire apparatus was cumbersome. Yet, the demonstration proved that the fundamental principles of colour transmission could be mastered. The system, known as **sequential colour television**, required three times the scanning information, demanding even greater bandwidth and increasing the technical difficulty exponentially. Despite these limitations, Baird's colour experiments were nearly two decades ahead of commercial colour broadcasting in the United States and the UK, demonstrating a breathtaking visionary scope and a capacity to solve problems using simple mechanical ingenuity where others were waiting for the arrival of advanced electronics. The successful demonstration of the Trichromatic Method further cemented Baird's reputation as the world's premier, if unorthodox, television pioneer.

6.4 The First Demonstration of Stereoscopic (3D) Television.

Baird's experiments were not confined to simply improving the two-dimensional, monochrome image; his mind was constantly seeking to exploit every possible dimension of visual communication. Following his successes in monochrome and colour, he turned his attention to adding **depth** to the televised image, resulting in the world's first demonstration of **stereoscopic or 3D television** in August 1928. This move underscored his belief that television must not merely replicate radio with pictures, but offer a wholly new and immersive visual experience.

The principle behind stereoscopic vision is to present a slightly different image to each eye, mimicking the way human vision perceives depth. Baird's solution, like his colour system, was purely mechanical and relied on synchronization and sequential presentation. To capture the images, the transmitter employed two distinct lenses, spaced approximately the same distance apart as human eyes, focused on the subject. Each lens captured a slightly different perspective of the scene.

These two perspectives were then scanned sequentially using a modified Nipkow disc. The disc featured two sets of scanning holes, one for the left-eye image and one for the right-eye image, transmitting the two separate signals one after the other. At the receiver end, the audience had to wear special viewing apparatus: **synchronizing shutters or coloured glasses** (the latter requiring two separate colour filters, such as red and cyan, one for each eye). The synchronized mechanical shutter system was the more technologically complex approach, flickering rapidly to ensure that the left eye only saw the left-eye image and the right eye only saw the right-eye image.

When viewed correctly, the crude 30-line images, now presented with binocular disparity, suddenly gained an astonishing sense of depth. The image appeared to leap out of the screen, creating a compelling, if unstable, 3D effect. The demonstration was a powerful theatrical statement, though it had no immediate commercial application due to the complexity required for the viewer. The need for special glasses or synchronized shutters, combined with the extreme flickering and low definition, made it impractical for the average home.

Despite the technical hurdles, the demonstration of 3D television was further proof of Baird's immense technological leapfrogging. He was consistently showing that the mechanical system was far more versatile and flexible than its critics believed. By demonstrating colour, 3D, and long-distance transmission within a short span, Baird presented a vision of television that was complete and comprehensive, forcing the world to recognize the medium's vast potential beyond simple black-and-white images.

6.5 International Expansion: Licensing and Demonstrations in Germany and the USA.

The relentless sequence of technical firsts—transatlantic, outdoor, colour, and 3D—fueled a rapid and aggressive international expansion campaign by the BTDC. Having demonstrated that the system worked, the company's next logical step was to license the technology abroad and establish a dominant global position before electronic rivals could gain traction. The two primary targets for this expansion were **Germany** and the **United States**, key markets with advanced scientific communities and massive potential consumer bases.

In Germany, Baird's technology found a highly receptive audience. The German government and its scientific institutions were deeply interested in adopting the emerging technology, and in 1928, a subsidiary company, **Fernseh AG**, was established. Fernseh AG was a collaboration between the BTDC, the German Post Office (Reichspost), and leading German firms like Zeiss Ikon and Bosch. This partnership was crucial; it gave the BTDC access to superior German engineering and manufacturing capabilities, allowing for the refinement of the Nipkow disc and associated equipment. Germany quickly became the site of some of the most intensive experimental broadcasting in Europe, firmly rooted in Baird's mechanical principles.

The American market, however, proved more volatile and challenging. In the USA, Baird formed the **Baird Television Corporation**, setting up demonstration labs in New York. The transatlantic broadcast had provided an ideal launchpad, and he began a series of high-profile demonstrations. However, the American landscape was dominated by large, well-funded electrical giants like **RCA, General Electric (GE), and Westinghouse**. These corporations, with massive research budgets, were already deeply committed to developing electronic television, led by inventors such as Vladimir Zworykin and Philo Farnsworth. The American industry viewed Baird's mechanical system as an outdated novelty, a charming but temporary distraction.

While Baird secured limited licenses and generated considerable public attention, the power of the American corporate opposition was immense. They controlled the press, held immense sway with regulatory bodies, and could afford to wait for their higher-definition electronic systems to mature. Baird's US expansion was a commercial and legal battleground, forcing him to defend his patents and his low-definition system against the promise of electronic superiority. Despite the intense resistance, by the end of 1929, the BTDC had successfully planted flags in key international territories, establishing Baird's mechanical television as a globally recognized, commercially active, and technically proven system, even as the seeds of its electronic successor were already being sown across the ocean.

Chapter 7: The BBC and the Zenith of Mechanical TV (1929–1932)

7.1 Collaboration with the British Broadcasting Corporation (BBC) for Trial Broadcasts.

The most critical moment in John Logie Baird's career—the turning point that propelled his invention from a sensational laboratory demonstration into a public service—came through the complex and often antagonistic relationship he developed with the British Broadcasting Corporation. For years, Baird and the representatives of the Baird Television Development Company (BTDC) had engaged in a sustained and aggressive lobbying campaign against the staunch conservatism of the BBC's founding visionary, Sir John Reith. Reith held a powerful, almost proprietary view of public broadcasting, seeing it as a moral and educational instrument intended for the betterment of the nation. He viewed television, particularly in its rudimentary 30-line form, as an inherently trivial, low-brow technology that would cheapen the quality and purpose of sound radio. His official stance was one of deep, philosophical skepticism, which translated into a formidable bureaucratic resistance against allowing the disruptive technology access to the BBC's infrastructure. Baird's persistence was legendary, and he understood that the scientific marvel was worthless without a transmission conduit of national reach.

The impasse was finally broken not by Reith's consent, but by the intervention of a higher regulatory power: the General Post Office (GPO), which held authority over all wireless communication licenses in the United Kingdom. The GPO's technical experts recognized the international prestige and scientific value of Baird's achievement, and they were keen to ensure that Britain, as the birthplace of television, retained its technological lead. Following immense political pressure, journalistic excitement, and several compelling public exhibitions that demonstrated the undeniable workability of the system, the GPO effectively mandated the BBC's involvement. The resultant agreement, hammered out in 1929, was a political compromise designed to satisfy all parties while maintaining the BBC's distance. The BBC would not incorporate television into its standard schedule but would permit trial transmissions. These were strictly defined as experimental, confined to times when they would not interrupt the main radio schedule—typically late at night, after the conclusion of the serious cultural programming—and were explicitly non-commercial.

The BTDC was made responsible for everything related to the visual signal: supplying, installing, operating, and maintaining all the vision equipment, and producing the content. The BBC's contribution was the immense power of its long-wave radio transmitter at Brookmans Park and the infrastructure to handle the audio signal. This separation of duties, where the BBC provided the established airwaves and Baird provided the volatile new technology, was a practical solution that limited the BBC's risk while granting Baird the essential legitimacy he needed. In September 1929, the first official trial broadcasts began, marking the formal inauguration of the world's first regularly scheduled public television service. This achievement was a triumph of engineering demonstration and political maneuver, a hard-won entry that placed mechanical television firmly onto the public agenda, despite the institutionally rooted opposition it faced.

7.2 Installation of Baird Equipment at the BBC's Savoy Hill Studios.

The physical implementation of the television service required the installation of Baird's unique apparatus within the heart of the BBC's main London headquarters, the Savoy Hill Studios. This installation was a profound juxtaposition of old and new technology, creating immediate and significant operational conflicts. The BBC studios were painstakingly designed for acoustic perfection; every soundproofing measure and microphone placement was intended to capture the highest fidelity of the human voice and musical performance. Baird's mechanical system, in contrast, was defined by noise, heat, and intense, bright light, which created immense challenges for harmonious cohabitation.

The centerpiece of the transmission apparatus was the Flying Spot Scanner. Unlike later electronic cameras, this was an entirely mechanical device. It worked by focusing a powerful lamp through the spiral of holes on a large, heavy, rapidly rotating Nipkow disc. This created a tiny, intense spot of light that mechanically swept, or scanned, the subject, line by line. The light reflected off the subject—a person's face, for instance—was not captured by an optical lens, but by large banks of photoelectric cells placed around the studio. These cells converted the minute changes in light intensity into the electrical video signal. The process was inherently difficult to manage. The electric motor spinning the disc produced a constant, penetrating whine, and the subjects had to endure a searing glare from the necessary illumination, which was far brighter than standard studio lighting.

To cope with the inevitable noise pollution, the Baird equipment was often housed in a separate, isolated chamber or room, sometimes a floor above the main radio studio. This physical separation was essential because the BBC's sensitive audio microphones could not be allowed to pick up the mechanical noise of the scanner, which would ruin the simultaneous sound broadcast. Furthermore, the 30-line system was extremely unforgiving of movement. Performers had to be positioned with meticulous precision, often guided by marks on the floor or even subtle head restraints, to ensure their face remained centered within the tiny, effective scanning area. This area was often no more than a few square inches. The technical staff were faced with the daily challenge of maintaining perfect synchronization between the mechanical disc's speed and the electrical signal generated, while simultaneously ensuring the audio and video signals were perfectly coordinated for the listener at home.

The Savoy Hill installation was a temporary, improvised arrangement that revealed the inherent difficulties of the mechanical era. It demanded that the BBC's established radio engineers master a complex, unfamiliar, and temperamental system, dealing with its flickering neon light sources, managing the heat it generated, and constantly compensating for the motor's speed variations. This delicate and often volatile partnership, however, was the essential foundation upon which the world's first scheduled television service was built, integrating Baird's breakthrough into the authoritative framework of the national broadcaster.

7.3 Broadcast Schedules and the Content of Early 30-Line Television Programs.

The implementation of the trial broadcasts was tightly controlled by the BBC, resulting in a schedule that underscored the experimental and secondary nature of the medium. The transmissions commenced in September 1929, initially occurring only three days a week, and almost invariably took place late in the evening. The scheduling was a direct reflection of Sir John Reith's protective philosophy, as the transmissions were carefully slotted into the post-11 p.m. time slot, ensuring no interference with or cannibalization of the prime-time radio audience. This late-night hour immediately limited the potential viewing audience to the most dedicated hobbyists and night owls.

The programs themselves were rigidly dictated by the severe technical constraints of the 30-line picture. The extremely low resolution—a mere thirty scan lines—meant the image could only convey general shape and tone, lacking the detail to show full-body action or wide sets. Consequently, all programming had to be presented in extreme close-up. The performers' entire repertoire was limited to simple head-and-shoulders shots, or even just the face, which required a complete re-thinking of performance. Movement was the enemy of the 30-line system; the slow frame rate, typically around 12.5 frames per second, rendered any quick motion into an unwatchable, abstract smear. Performers were rigorously coached to move slowly, deliberately, or often remain perfectly still, relying primarily on subtle facial expressions to convey emotion or meaning.

The typical content reflected these technical limitations: simple "talking head" presentations, brief monologues by actors, or appearances by prominent public figures who were willing to sit still under the glaring lights. Musicians and singers would perform, but their physical performance was secondary to the sheer wonder of seeing their faces move. Short, carefully rehearsed dramatic sketches were a staple, utilizing simple props and highly restricted movement. To aid in focusing and testing the scanner, simple objects or models were frequently used, such as the instantly recognizable Baird 'Gnome,' a simple stylized face that became an accidental icon of the early broadcasts. This necessity for minimal motion often led to amusing anecdotes of actors attempting to scratch an itch or shift their weight without ruining the entire transmission.

The viewing experience was inherently complex due to the requirement for separate audio and vision signals. The sound was broadcast on the BBC's powerful long-wave radio transmitter, while the video signal was sent on a separate, shortwave radio frequency. This meant the viewer required two pieces of equipment—a standard radio for the sound, and a Televisor unit for the picture—which had to be tuned and synchronized manually. The early scheduled broadcasts, despite their crudity and inconvenience, marked a genuine breakthrough, establishing Britain as the world leader in regular public television service and forcing the development of early, constrained content formats.

7.4 The Launch of Commercial Televisors for Home Use.

The commencement of regular BBC trial broadcasts created an immediate, if highly specialized, consumer demand. The Baird Television Development Company (BTDC) quickly moved to capitalize on this, launching the first commercially produced television receiver for the home, branded the Televisor. The existence of a dedicated receiving apparatus that could be purchased and installed by the general public was crucial; it legitimized television as more than just a laboratory curiosity and established it as a viable consumer electronic product, albeit one targeted at an elite, technically literate audience.

The Televisor was an ingenious piece of mechanical engineering encased in a simple, rectangular wooden cabinet, designed to sit next to the purchaser's existing shortwave radio set. Its mechanism was straightforward: an electric motor drove a spinning metal disc that was an exact replica of the scanning disc used at the transmission end. The image itself was created by a bright, reddish-orange neon lamp positioned behind the disc. The incoming video signal modulated the intensity of the neon light, and as the disc rotated, the flashes of light were viewed through a small magnifying lens or aperture on the front of the cabinet. The resulting picture was tiny, typically only two by three inches, monochromatic, and characterized by a persistent, noticeable flicker due to the low frame rate.

Operating the Televisor was an interactive, highly technical process that demanded the user's full attention and skill. This was far from the simple "switch on and watch" experience of the future. The most difficult and critical task was synchronization. The viewer had to manually adjust the motor's speed—often using a precise variable resistor or rheostat—until the rotation of the disc in their living room exactly matched the speed of the disc spinning miles away at the Savoy Hill studio. If the speed was slightly off, the image would scroll, tear, or distort uncontrollably, appearing as abstract bands of light and dark. Once the image was stable, the viewer then had to simultaneously tune in their separate radio set to the BBC's long-wave frequency to receive the corresponding audio.

The price of the Televisor, around twenty-five guineas, ensured that the initial market was small, comprising wealthy enthusiasts and dedicated radio hobbyists. However, the commercial offering generated immense interest beyond the buyers. Detailed plans and technical specifications were published in popular wireless magazines, inspiring a vibrant community of amateur constructors who built their own "homebrew" receivers using repurposed parts, lenses, and electric motors. This activity validated Baird's design philosophy: the mechanical nature of the Televisor made it accessible, reproducible, and repairable, creating a grassroots movement that firmly established mechanical television as a commercial reality.

7.5 The Consolidation of Mechanical Television as the World Standard.

By the beginning of the 1930s, the 30-line mechanical system, spearheaded by John Logie Baird and his company, had successfully captured a unique and significant global position: it was recognized as the world's only operational standard for regular public television broadcasting. The practical, working partnership established with the BBC served as a powerful model that was swiftly emulated internationally. Baird's technology and licensing agreements facilitated the establishment of similar experimental and trial services in nations across Europe, including Germany through the subsidiary Fernseh AG, and in France and the United States, where his apparatus was used in various high-profile technical demonstrations.

This global dominance was largely due to the system's immediate practicality and simplicity. While leading figures in electronic television, such as Philo Farnsworth in the U.S. and Vladimir Zworykin under the vast research umbrella of RCA, were making revolutionary strides toward high-definition electronic scanning, their methods remained complex, expensive, and largely confined to tightly controlled laboratory environments. Baird's system, relying on mechanical ingenuity, was robust, relatively inexpensive to produce, and—most importantly—it worked reliably over broadcast distances and could be received by a consumer-friendly, if rudimentary, device like the Televisor. The fact that the British state broadcaster had adopted it for a scheduled service conferred an unmatched level of public and institutional legitimacy, momentarily placing the mechanical method at the apex of the field.

This period, therefore, represents the high point and ultimate validation of Baird's low-definition work. His company, the BTDC, enjoyed success, prestige, and a clear path toward commercial expansion. They had a proven technology, an established market, and an official blessing. However, this very success harbored the seeds of future decline. The focus on commercializing the existing 30-line system led to an institutional reluctance to commit the massive capital and research required to fundamentally rethink the technology. The immense difficulty and physical limitations inherent in driving the mechanical system toward higher resolution were being steadily, silently surpassed by the purely electronic methods being developed elsewhere.

The 30-line standard had consolidated the world market, but it simultaneously masked the exponential progress being made by electronic rivals. While Baird himself was exploring hybrid solutions, often combining a mechanical camera with a far superior electronic cathode ray tube (CRT) receiver, the commercially available product and the broadcasting standard remained firmly rooted in the low-definition mechanical principle. This consolidation of the market marked the zenith of mechanical television just as the inevitable technological shift toward electronic scanning was gathering insurmountable momentum, positioning the Baird company for a dramatic and devastating confrontation with an entirely new wave of innovation.

Chapter 8: The Shadow of Electronic Television (1932–1935)

8.1 The Financial and Technical Troubles of the Baird Company

By the early 1930s, the initial euphoria surrounding John Logie Baird's achievement of genuine television had begun to curdle into a grim reality of commercial and technical inadequacy. The Baird Television Development Company, despite its pioneering status and constant stream of publicity, was structurally unsound. Its revenues were minimal, derived mostly from the sale of rudimentary 30-line receiving sets and the occasional large-screen theatrical demonstration, rather than from a sustained, profitable business model. The company was perpetually hungry for capital, relying on enthusiastic but increasingly anxious investors who had been promised a technological revolution and the resulting financial windfall. This required Baird himself to spend considerable time in the boardroom, away from the laboratory, attempting to reassure financial backers and fend off persistent shareholder demands for tangible results and dividend payouts.

The technical specifications of the current system were a primary source of this financial strain. The 30-line system, while remarkable for its time, offered a picture that was barely more than a flickering silhouette, limited by the physics of the spinning Nipkow disc. The images were small, suffered from severe flicker, and lacked the detail necessary to hold the public imagination beyond novelty. Furthermore, the transmission of the low-definition signal required a significant bandwidth commitment from the BBC—a commitment that the public broadcaster, increasingly aware of the limitations and the emerging competition, was reluctant to expand. The inherent inefficiency meant the company was spending vast sums on maintaining a service that provided a poor user experience, a situation that terrified the accountants.

Baird's public demonstrations, often involving spectacular large-screen projections, were designed to mask the deficiency of the home receivers. While these events generated headlines and briefly boosted share prices, they were expensive and unsustainable as a long-term commercial strategy. They fostered a disconnect between the public's perception of television's potential (as seen in a cinema) and the actual performance of the product available for purchase. This gap eroded public confidence, making mass adoption impossible. The engineers understood that 30 lines was a technological cul-de-sac; any meaningful progress demanded a leap in definition, which mechanical scanning apparatus was fundamentally unsuited to deliver without becoming impossibly large, noisy, and complex.

Moreover, the company's patent portfolio, while extensive, was centred on mechanical principles that were rapidly becoming obsolete. The real value of the company lay in Baird's genius and the goodwill associated with the invention, but goodwill does not pay the salaries of a growing engineering staff or fund the development of high-definition apparatus. The structure was further complicated by the division of responsibilities: Baird was the inventor and visionary, but he often clashed with the pragmatic businessmen brought in to manage the operations, creating internal friction that slowed down crucial development decisions. The financial pressures were compounded by the ticking clock of technological evolution, pushing the company into increasingly desperate and costly ventures to maintain its lead.

The low definition also created significant limitations on the type of content that could be broadcast. Only close-ups of faces, hands, or very simple motion were intelligible, restricting television to brief, static performances or spoken word transmissions, which the BBC eventually curtailed to off-peak hours. This lack of compelling programming further depressed receiver sales, creating a vicious cycle of low investment leading to low quality, which in turn led to low demand. By 1933, the company was running on fumes, sustained more by the monumental reputation of its founder than by any concrete hope of imminent profitability, all while a far more robust, future-proof technology was being perfected just down the road. The Baird Company had achieved the impossible by creating television, but it was now financially and technically unable to capitalize on its own invention in a competitive marketplace.

The need to perpetually innovate to justify investment led to the pursuit of increasingly exotic and technically fraught solutions, like colour and stereoscopic television, sometimes at the expense of perfecting the fundamental monochromatic service. These demonstrations, while showcasing Baird's undeniable brilliance and relentless inventive spirit, did little to address the core problem: the requirement for a cheap, reliable, and high-definition system suitable for mass production and domestic viewing. The reliance on a system of whirling physical components had reached its practical and economic limit, leaving the company vulnerable to any competitor offering a solution based on pure physics and electronics.

8.2 The Growing Threat from EMI/Marconi and the Electronic (Cathode Ray Tube) System

The real, existential threat to the Baird Company did not come from other mechanical pioneers, but from the industrial and technological might of a collaboration that would ultimately define the future of television: the merger between the Electrical and Musical Industries (EMI) and the wireless communications titan, Marconi. This fusion, completed in the early 1930s, created a technological powerhouse with vast financial resources, an immense patent library, and a deep bench of scientific talent, crucially led by the brilliant engineer Isaac Shoenberg. While Baird's method was the culmination of nineteenth-century mechanical invention, the EMI/Marconi approach was firmly rooted in the twentieth century's electronic revolution.

The core difference lay in the method of scanning and display. Baird relied on spinning discs, mirrors, or drums—physical components that had inertia, made noise, and were limited in speed and precision by manufacturing tolerances. EMI/Marconi, however, adopted the Cathode Ray Tube (CRT) system. Developed by Vladimir Zworykin and Philo Farnsworth in the United States, and significantly refined by the EMI team in Britain, the CRT system scanned and displayed the image entirely by using electron beams, with no moving parts. The camera—or "eye" of the system—was the Emitron tube, a sophisticated device that converted light directly into electrical signals with high efficiency and precision.

The advantages of the electronic system were immediately apparent and insurmountable. Firstly, definition was limited only by the electronics, not by the size of a motor or the number of holes on a disc. This meant high-definition—initially 405 lines—could be achieved almost immediately and easily upgraded later, far surpassing the best possible mechanical standard. Secondly, the electronic display produced a bright, stable, and completely flicker-free image, unlike the dim and shimmering output of the mechanical screen. Thirdly, the silence of the electronic receiver was a massive benefit over the whirring sound of a 30-line mechanical box. Finally, the electronic system offered superior light sensitivity, meaning broadcasts could move beyond studio close-ups to cover external scenes and larger, more complex studio productions, which was essential for compelling programming.

The BBC, which had been patient with Baird's 30-line transmissions, was growing increasingly impatient with the mechanical system's limitations. They understood that the future of broadcasting lay in high-fidelity, high-definition images that could compete with cinema and radio, not simply supplement them. When EMI demonstrated their early high-definition electronic system in secret, the contrast with Baird's technology was startling. Shoenberg's team was not merely offering a better picture; they were offering a fundamentally different and superior technological paradigm, one that had the capacity for true mass-market adoption and development.

EMI/Marconi's strategy was not based on public stunts but on rigorous, scientific development and the acquisition of key patents, creating a fortress of intellectual property around electronic television. They developed their own version of the CRT camera, the Emitron, and secured licenses for crucial American patents, ensuring their system was comprehensive and legally protected. This corporate strength, combined with the clear technical superiority of the electronic method, put the Baird Company, which had relied on the brilliance of a single inventor and limited funding, at a severe disadvantage. The shadow cast by electronic television was long and deep, signalling the inevitable obsolescence of Baird's pioneering, but ultimately historical, system.

8.3 Baird's Response: Developing Intermediate Film (IF) and High-Definition Mechanical Systems

Faced with the undeniable technical lead of the EMI/Marconi electronic system, John Logie Baird and his engineers mounted a vigorous, two-pronged counterattack, demonstrating his characteristic tenacity and ingenious inventiveness. His response was to pivot sharply toward high-definition solutions, accepting that the low-definition 30-line era was over. The first prong of this strategy was the Intermediate Film (IF) system, and the second was the development of higher-line mechanical scanners, specifically aiming for a 240-line standard.

The Intermediate Film system, introduced around 1932, was Baird's most successful stopgap measure for achieving high-definition studio broadcasts using mechanical methods. The concept was remarkably convoluted but effective: live performers were filmed by a motion-picture camera in a darkened, sound-proof booth. The developed film, still wet from the chemical bath, was then rushed down a series of tubes to a scanning chamber where it was scanned by a high-intensity light source. The resulting high-definition image signal was then broadcast. This system allowed Baird to demonstrate images of up to 120 lines, and later higher, that were dramatically better than the live 30-line broadcast. While this method provided a crucial, temporary way to match the clarity of the emerging electronic displays in public demonstrations, it was fraught with logistical and technical nightmares.

The process of capturing, processing, and scanning film required a constant supply of chemicals, was noisy, and introduced a 45 to 60-second delay between the live action and the broadcast image, making live broadcasting in the true sense of the word impossible. It was a brilliant, but ultimately impractical, hybrid of cinema and television, demonstrating Baird's ability to invent around a problem but also highlighting the profound limitations of the mechanical approach. It was a technological compromise, a Rube Goldberg device designed to satisfy the demand for better definition until a purely mechanical high-definition system could be perfected.

Simultaneously, Baird pushed his engineering team to evolve the mechanical scanning apparatus itself. The trusty Nipkow disc was deemed obsolete for anything above 90 lines due to its enormous required size and rotational speed. Instead, the focus shifted to the mirror drum and, later, the mirror screw. The mirror drum was a cylinder with a series of accurately angled small mirrors around its circumference. As the drum spun, each mirror scanned a thin horizontal strip of the image. By increasing the number of mirrors and the speed of rotation, higher line counts, such as the target of 240 lines, could theoretically be achieved. The mirror screw was an even more complex arrangement of accurately cut, tilted surfaces.

However, scaling these mechanical systems was an engineering nightmare. High-definition scanning required extraordinary precision. Any minute deviation in the angle or positioning of a mirror led to noticeable distortions and jitter in the received picture. The parts needed to spin at ferocious speeds, causing vibration, noise, and rapid wear, and demanding powerful motors. Despite these challenges, the development of the 240-line mechanical standard, often relying on the mirror drum for scanning and projection, was the second critical pillar of Baird's defense strategy. He was betting that the cost and complexity of the EMI electronic system would delay its readiness, giving his hybrid and mechanical high-definition efforts a temporary window to become the established standard.

8.4 The Failure to Achieve a Viable High-Definition Mechanical Standard (240 lines)

The push to establish the 240-line mechanical standard represented the final, desperate gamble for John Logie Baird and the company that bore his name. By 1934, it was clear that only a definition of 200 lines or more would be considered acceptable for a national public service. The Baird team selected 240 lines, using a sequential scanning method at 25 frames per second, which required a significant jump in technological capability from their previous 30-line transmissions. However, the attempt to force mechanical technology into the high-definition domain ultimately proved to be a practical and economic failure.

The core problem lay in the physics of scale. A mechanical device capable of scanning 240 lines required components of such precise manufacture, and spinning at such high speeds, that the system was prone to inherent faults. The mirror drums, while superior to the Nipkow disc for high line counts, were extremely sensitive to vibration. The smallest mechanical imperfection resulted in 'banding' or 'hunting'—a visible, unstable quality in the televised image. The engineering tolerances required to maintain stability at the necessary rotational speed were prohibitively expensive and difficult to meet consistently in mass production, suggesting that even if a prototype worked flawlessly in the laboratory, reliable, high-volume manufacturing would be impossible.

Furthermore, the light source and light sensitivity remained a challenge. To capture the full detail of a 240-line image, the mechanical scanner needed incredibly bright illumination at the transmitting end, and the receiver required a robust light valve or projection system.

The light sources available for mechanical scanning were simply not efficient enough to produce a bright, large image without excessive heat and power consumption. While the Intermediate Film system offered temporary relief for studio work, the search for a direct, high-definition mechanical camera remained elusive, especially one that could rival the instantaneous light sensitivity of the new EMI Emitron camera tube.

In contrast, the electronic system offered a simple, stable solution. The EMI team, under Shoenberg, had successfully demonstrated a 405-line system with interlaced scanning, providing a vastly superior image with no mechanical noise, no flicker, and crucially, no moving parts. The comparison between the two systems was damning. Baird's 240-line mechanical display—often using projection optics to enlarge the image—was clearly unstable, noisy, and provided a picture that was only marginally better than his own previous efforts, while the electronic 405-line image, displayed on a stable CRT, was bright, clear, and looked like the future.

The Baird Company found itself cornered. It had invested heavily in a technology that had reached its practical zenith, attempting to compete on definition with a technology that had only just begun its exponential development curve. The limitations of the 240-line mechanical system, especially its poor performance in capturing outdoor scenes or anything beyond a bright studio, ultimately convinced the decision-makers that the Baird system could not form the basis of a sustainable national broadcasting service. The reliance on Intermediate Film for any quality content was perceived as a clear admission that the mechanical system was inadequate for truly live, high-definition television.

8.5 Government Intervention: The Appointment of the Television Committee

The technical impasse between the Baird Company's mechanical system and the EMI/Marconi electronic system could not be solved by market forces alone. As both companies prepared to demonstrate competing, incompatible high-definition standards, the British government realized that a crucial decision had to be made about the future of national public service broadcasting. The BBC, which would be tasked with operating the service, urgently required a single, universal standard to avoid costly dual transmissions and confusion among manufacturers and consumers. This necessity led to one of the most significant governmental interventions in the history of broadcasting: the appointment of the Television Committee in May 1934.

Chaired by Lord Selsdon, the Committee's mandate was explicit and wide-ranging: to consider the development of television systems, determine the criteria for a high-definition public service, and recommend which system or systems should be adopted as the national standard for the United Kingdom. This was a direct response to the situation where two technically distinct, high-definition solutions—Baird's 240-line mechanical/IF hybrid and EMI/Marconi's 405-line electronic system—were vying for the privilege of establishing the standard for a technology with incalculable social and economic potential. The government correctly judged that leaving the choice to commercial rivalry would result in chaos, delaying the introduction of television for years.

The Committee spent nearly a year gathering evidence, consulting with engineers, and examining demonstrations from both the Baird and

EMI/Marconi groups, as well as considering other international developments. The engineers, including those from the BBC, provided crucial testimony regarding the practicalities, reliability, and costs of operating both systems. While Baird's pioneering spirit and continuous innovation were praised, the weight of the technical evidence tilted heavily in favour of the electronic solution. The committee's experts recognized that the electronic CRT system offered a clearer path to future development, greater picture quality, and superior reliability.

The Committee released its report in January 1935, which proved to be a pivotal moment. The conclusion was a masterful political compromise that, while appearing to give both companies a chance, ultimately sealed the fate of mechanical television. The report recommended that the BBC should launch a high-definition television service in London. Crucially, it recommended a side-by-side trial of the two competing systems from a single transmitter station at Alexandra Palace. The service would use the Baird 240-line mechanical system on one week and the EMI 405-line electronic system on the alternate week, allowing for a thorough and public comparison of the merits of each.

This decision was designed to be politically neutral, but the details of the trial were inherently challenging for the Baird Company. They were compelled to rapidly scale up their 240-line mechanical apparatus for continuous, broadcast-quality operation under intense scrutiny. Furthermore, the selection of the BBC's engineers to run the technical aspects of the service meant that the electronic system, which was fundamentally simpler and more robust to operate, would likely have an advantage. The trial was scheduled to begin in 1936, but the appointment of the Television Committee in 1934 had already initiated the shift of power, signaling that the era of mechanical television was drawing to a close and that the future belonged to the electron. The final countdown had begun.

8.6 The Initial Planning and Preparations for the Alexandra Palace Trial

The recommendation by the Selsdon Committee for a competitive, side-by-side trial at Alexandra Palace set off a frantic period of planning, engineering, and construction for both the Baird and EMI/Marconi teams. Alexandra Palace, a Victorian exhibition hall with two distinctive radio masts, was chosen as the ideal location for the world's first high-definition television transmitting station. Its elevated position in North London provided the necessary height for the antennae, and the large interior spaces were converted into two entirely separate, self-contained television studios and control rooms, one for each rival system.

For the Baird Television Company, this was a last-ditch attempt to prove the viability of their mechanical technology on a grand, national scale. Their preparation focused on making the 240-line mechanical system—and its reliance on the Intermediate Film method for high-quality studio work—as reliable and stable as possible. They knew the electronic system's image quality would be difficult to beat, so their strategy was to demonstrate stability, ease of use, and a commitment to innovation, even attempting to incorporate colour and stereoscopic elements into the broadcast schedule to wow the public and the BBC. The Baird studio suite had to accommodate the bulky Intermediate Film apparatus, with its tanks of developer and continuous film loops, alongside the necessary lighting and control equipment for the mechanical scanners.

The pressure on the engineers was immense. They had to transition from laboratory demonstrations to broadcast-grade operation in a matter of months, under the constant threat of failure. The financial burden was also staggering, requiring another significant injection of capital into a company already heavily indebted. John Logie Baird himself, while the figurehead, was by this point less involved in the day-to-day engineering details, having devolved much of the complex industrial development to his technical directors. Yet, his influence and reputation remained the company's biggest asset, and he frequently visited the site to spur on the workers.

In contrast, the EMI/Marconi team approached the challenge with clinical industrial efficiency. Their 405-line, 50-frames-per-second interlaced electronic system was fundamentally more robust. Their main preparation centred on optimizing the Emitron camera and its associated electronics, ensuring signal clarity and reliability. Their studio setup was simpler and cleaner, relying on the compact camera tubes and conventional studio lighting, without the need for the elaborate plumbing and chemistry of the Intermediate Film process. This allowed them to focus on the subtleties of electronic image production, such as achieving deeper blacks and higher contrast, which they knew would be the deciding factors in a side-by-side comparison.

The BBC acted as the neutral organizing body, responsible for building the shared infrastructure, including the massive transmitter itself, and for staffing the studios with production personnel. They adopted a dual-control-room approach, ensuring fair play by having separate engineering teams for each system. However, many BBC engineers were already convinced of the electronic system's superiority, which created a subtle, yet pervasive, psychological advantage for the EMI team. The construction and installation phase at Alexandra Palace were effectively a race against time, a technological showdown set against the ornate backdrop of a Victorian pleasure palace. The entire broadcasting world watched as two profoundly different technological philosophies—mechanical ingenuity versus electronic physics—prepared to clash for the right to establish the first national television standard. The stakes could not have been higher.

Chapter 9: The Alexandra Palace Trials and Defeat (1936–1937)

9.1 The Decision to Hold a Side-by-Side Comparison Trial by the BBC

The recommendation put forth by the Selsdon Committee in January 1935—that the BBC should conduct a competitive, side-by-side trial of the two leading high-definition television systems—was unprecedented in broadcasting history. It was a politically masterful solution to a complex technological deadlock. The British government, unwilling to risk backing a single standard that might quickly prove inferior, opted for an open competition, shifting the burden of the final decision from political bodies to engineering pragmatism. The BBC, specifically designated as the implementing authority, was tasked with establishing the world's first regular high-definition television service based on the outcome of this contest.

Alexandra Palace, nicknamed 'Ally Pally' by Londoners, was selected as the site for the new transmitting station. Its location on a high ridge in North London provided an excellent line of sight for broadcasting across a wide metropolitan area, an essential requirement for the trial. Within the palace's vast, ornate structure, the BBC constructed two entirely separate, self-contained studio complexes, known colloquially as the 'Baird side' and the 'EMI side.' This separation was crucial, allowing each company's team to operate its unique technology without interference, creating a truly fair ground for comparison. The BBC itself provided the centralized transmitter, the antennae, and the production staff who would alternate between the two studios.

The stakes could not have been higher. For the Baird Television Development Company, this trial was their final opportunity to secure the official government standard and validate the years of mechanical development spearheaded by John Logie Baird. Winning meant not only securing the contracts for the national service but also validating

Baird's lifetime belief in his original technological approach. Failure, conversely, meant financial ruin for the company and the technological relegation of its pioneering inventor. For EMI-Marconi, winning meant cementing their financial dominance in a new industry and validating their vast investment in electronic research, securing the technological future.

The BBC's decision to mandate a clear and continuous trial period, with the two systems operating on alternate weeks, was driven by the need for objective operational data. They needed to assess not just the quality of the image produced in a perfect demonstration, but the systems' reliability, running costs, ease of maintenance, and ability to handle diverse studio productions. This focus on operational efficiency was a critical turning point. While Baird's system could be made to look good during special events, its true test would be sustaining six hours of broadcast quality content every day. The meticulous planning by the BBC engineering department ensured that the transition between the two entirely incompatible systems could be managed cleanly, allowing the public and, more importantly, the BBC's internal engineering committee, to make a definitive judgement. The opening of the trial service on November 2, 1936, marked the definitive start of the contest that would determine the direction of television for the next half-century.

9.2 The Rival Systems: Baird's Improved Mechanical/IF System vs. the EMI-Marconi Electronic System

The two systems that faced off at Alexandra Palace in 1936 represented a fundamental schism in technological philosophy: the culmination of mechanical engineering versus the birth of pure electronics.

The Baird system, transmitting at a definition of 240 lines, utilized sequential scanning at 25 frames per second. Its strength lay in its ability to adapt proven cinematic techniques. For live studio broadcasts, the Baird team heavily relied on the Intermediate Film, or IF, system. This complex process involved performers being shot by a high-speed motion picture camera. The exposed film was then rapidly developed, fixed, washed, and dried in a continuous process involving chemical baths and pipes, before being scanned by a high-definition mechanical mirror-drum or mirror-screw apparatus. The scanned image signal was then transmitted. While IF offered a high-quality picture that could theoretically rival electronic output, it was cumbersome, messy, loud, and introduced a time delay of nearly a minute between the action and the broadcast, rendering genuine 'live' television impossible. Baird's team also demonstrated some fully mechanical scanning for certain studio items, using a massive, high-speed mirror-drum, but this apparatus struggled with illumination and image stability. For film material, they used a telecine system, which again employed a mechanical scanner to read the film frame by frame.

In stark contrast, the EMI-Marconi system was a purely electronic wonder, operating at 405 lines with an interlaced scanning method at 50 frames per second. The interlacing technique—splitting each frame into two fields of 202.5 lines—effectively doubled the apparent refresh rate, resulting in a virtually flicker-free picture, a massive advantage over the sequential 25-frame Baird system. The heart of the EMI system was the Emitron camera tube, a descendant of the technology developed by Zworykin and Farnsworth, which captured the scene using an electron beam without any moving parts. The advantages were profound: instant, true live coverage, quiet operation, and crucially, immense light sensitivity. The Emitron could function in relatively low light, giving producers far greater flexibility, whereas the Baird mirror-drum required punishingly intense illumination to generate a sufficient signal.

The difference in the output picture quality was immediately evident to observers. The EMI 405-line signal, viewed on a cathode ray tube receiver, was bright, stable, and sharp, defining a new standard for definition and realism. The Baird 240-line image, whether from the Intermediate Film or the mechanical scanner, often suffered from banding, jitter, and a general lack of stability inherent in high-speed mechanical components. The battle was between a magnificent, perfected 19th-century invention and a clean, futuristic 20th-century technology. The electronic system offered higher definition, higher frame rate, greater stability, and true immediacy, forcing the Baird system to rely on Rube Goldberg-esque workarounds that were ultimately unsustainable for a public broadcasting service.

9.3 Technical Differences and Operational Challenges of the Two Systems

The operational reality inside Alexandra Palace quickly revealed the profound gulf between the two competing technologies. The technical differences translated directly into massive disparities in operational efficiency, reliability, and cost—factors that proved decisive in the BBC's final recommendation.

The Baird studio was an industrial environment, dominated by the Intermediate Film machinery. This included a series of large, interconnected tanks containing developing, fixing, and washing solutions, all of which had to be temperature-controlled and constantly replenished. The entire IF system required dedicated chemical engineers and complex logistics for managing the film stock and processing fluids. The running of this apparatus was noisy and introduced a significant delay, restricting director spontaneity. Furthermore, the IF system was a single point of failure; if the film jammed, or the chemistry failed, the entire live broadcast stopped. The mechanical scanning equipment, when used directly, was also a challenge. The whirling mirror-drums required intricate maintenance, and their inherent noise often bled into the microphone pick-up, despite the acoustic separation of the camera room. The system was, in short, extremely high-maintenance and offered low operational tolerance for error.

The EMI-Marconi studio, by contrast, resembled a modern film set. It was clean, quiet, and required only the camera operators, lighting technicians, and standard vision control engineers. The Emitron camera tubes, while expensive, were solid-state devices with no moving parts to wear out. The system was inherently reliable and offered instant operational readiness. A director could call for an instantaneous cut or pan without fear of mechanical failure or chemical delays. The electronic system's superior light sensitivity also reduced the heat generated in the studio, making conditions far more comfortable for performers and crew, and allowing for greater flexibility in lighting designs and staging.

The cost analysis was equally damning for Baird. While the initial capital outlay for the complex electronic gear was significant, the long-term running costs of the EMI system were lower due to its superior reliability and lower maintenance needs. The Baird system, with its constant need for film, processing chemicals, and specialized mechanical maintenance staff, incurred high daily operational expenditures. Reliability was the final nail in the coffin. Throughout the trial, the EMI-Marconi system was noted for its consistent, trouble-free performance. The Baird broadcasts, while occasionally achieving spectacular results, were plagued by frequent breakdowns and disruptions caused by mechanical failures, film jams, and synchronization issues. The BBC, focused on delivering a stable, reliable public service, could not ignore the operational fragility of the mechanical system.

The BBC engineers, the primary users of the equipment, were overwhelmingly in favour of the electronic solution. Their collective feedback, rooted in daily practical experience, was the most powerful evidence presented to the decision-makers, validating the technological supremacy of the electronic cathode ray tube over the ingenuity of mechanical optics.

9.4 The Government's Decision to Adopt the EMI-Marconi System

The competitive trial at Alexandra Palace officially ran from November 1936. The service schedule mandated that one week would be dedicated exclusively to the Baird 240-line transmissions, followed by a week dedicated to the EMI 405-line transmissions. This alternating schedule allowed manufacturers, the press, and the public to compare the systems directly. However, the operational reality of the competition soon made the outcome inevitable.

The superiority of the EMI-Marconi system was quickly recognized by almost all observers. The 405-line, interlaced picture, with its higher definition and complete lack of flicker, was visibly and technically superior to the Baird 240-line sequential image. Critically, the EMI system's reliability during continuous broadcasting was vastly better. The Baird team suffered several high-profile technical failures, including an incident where one of their main transmission cables caught fire, causing a lengthy service interruption. These incidents, while dramatic, underscored the operational risk inherent in relying on the high-speed mechanical and chemical processes of their system.

The BBC's Television Advisory Committee, which monitored the trial closely and compiled the final report, did not need to wait for the trial's scheduled end in early 1937 to reach its conclusion. The technical staff's feedback was uniform: the EMI system was more stable, offered a better picture, was less cumbersome to operate, and provided genuine 'live' capability, making it superior for public service broadcasting.

On January 29, 1937, a mere eleven weeks into the intended six-month trial, the Postmaster General announced the Government's definitive decision. The announcement stated that the Baird system would be dropped, and the BBC television service would henceforth operate solely using the EMI-Marconi 405-line electronic standard. The decision was final and irrevocable. It was a formal governmental endorsement of the electronic path and the definitive rejection of mechanical television as the basis for the national service.

For John Logie Baird, this decision was a crushing blow, representing the official end of his pioneering system's dominance in the field he had essentially created. The mechanical apparatus, the spinning discs, the drums, and the Intermediate Film processor, were to be silenced. The decision was not a dismissal of Baird's inventive genius—which was always acknowledged—but a hard-nosed, pragmatic choice based on technological evolution and the demands of large-scale public service infrastructure. The government had correctly identified the technology that offered the most promising future, leaving Baird, the inventor of television, on the sidelines of the industry he had founded.

9.5 The Immediate Aftermath and the End of the 30-Line Broadcasts

The government's decision in January 1937 brought immediate and painful consequences for the Baird Company and marked the end of the first, mechanical era of television broadcasting in Britain.

The most immediate change was at Alexandra Palace itself. The Baird studio, with its messy, noisy Intermediate Film machinery and complex mechanical scanners, was shut down. The infrastructure was dismantled, and the facility was consolidated into a single operation running exclusively on the EMI-Marconi electronic system. This swift transition underscored the finality of the decision. The BBC, having committed to the electronic standard, wasted no time in fully adopting the 405-line system, which offered a vastly superior and more reliable product for its nascent viewing audience.

Simultaneously, the decision sealed the fate of the original, rudimentary low-definition service. Since 1929, the BBC had broadcast Baird's experimental 30-line transmissions, initially from their radio transmitter and later from the BBC control room at Broadcasting House. These broadcasts, limited to off-peak hours and providing only the flickering silhouette images, had sustained the public's connection to television for seven years. The existence of a dedicated, high-definition service from Alexandra Palace made the continuation of the low-definition experiments obsolete. The 30-line transmissions ceased altogether, extinguishing the last flicker of Baird's pioneering mechanical standard from the airwaves.

John Logie Baird and the company he founded were left reeling. The stock price of Baird Television Development Company plummeted following the announcement. The company, facing the loss of its primary commercial validation and its exclusive association with the national service, had to execute a rapid and traumatic pivot. Baird himself, however, never stopped inventing. Far from retreating, he used the company's remaining resources to focus on areas where mechanical technology might still hold an edge, such as large-screen theatre television and, critically, the development of colour and three-dimensional systems. He recognized that while the battle for monochromatic home television was lost, the war for future television standards—in colour and in depth—was still open.

Despite the setback, the Alexandra Palace trial holds immense historical significance. It established the world's first regularly scheduled, high-definition television service and, through its clear-cut result, settled the debate between mechanical and electronic systems globally. The failure of Baird's system was not due to a lack of inventive brilliance or effort, but rather the hard reality that mechanical components could not compete with the speed, stability, and future potential of electron-beam technology. The end of the trial cemented the dominance of the electronic cathode ray tube and ushered in the modern age of broadcasting.

Chapter 10: Private Innovation During World War II (1937–1945)

10.1 Baird's Shift Away from Commercial Broadcast towards Specialized Innovation

The year 1937 was, in many respects, a point of inflection that nearly broke the spirit and the company of John Logie Baird. The formal adoption of the EMI-Marconi 405-line electronic standard as the national broadcasting system in January of that year was not just a technical verdict; it was a commercial and psychological blow of monumental proportions. Having single-handedly ushered television into the world, Baird found himself definitively exiled from the mainstream application of his own creation. The initial shock quickly gave way to a decisive strategic pivot. Baird, with characteristic resilience, recognized that the battle for domestic monochromatic television was lost, but the war for the technological future, particularly in specialized and advanced applications, remained wide open.

This shift saw Baird withdraw his company's focus almost entirely from mass-market receiver manufacturing and standard broadcast development. The Baird Television Development Company underwent a painful restructuring, shedding much of its staff and abandoning the costly pursuit of conventional broadcasting contracts. Instead, Baird directed the remaining engineers and capital toward areas where the complexity and scale of his mechanical and electro-mechanical systems could still compete, or where electronic solutions had not yet been fully realized. These niches were primarily large-screen theatre television and, more fundamentally, the perfection of colour and three-dimensional transmission—technologies far beyond the capabilities of the rudimentary 405-line system.

Baird's genius had always been in the conceptual leap, the ingenious, often brute-force application of physics to solve an intractable problem.

In the post-1937 era, this genius was applied to the extremely high-end of television technology. He saw that while the pure electronic system was superior for a small domestic screen, the mechanical mirror-drum or intermediate film techniques could still be adapted to project truly massive, bright images in a cinema setting, a feat still challenging for early cathode ray tubes. This specialization was not merely a retreat; it was an attempt to future-proof his work by targeting the most advanced and visually demanding applications, effectively betting on the limits of contemporary electronic engineering.

This period was also marked by a move toward greater personal involvement in the laboratory. The distraction of perpetually courting investors and defending the flawed 30-line system was largely over. Baird, who had been diagnosed with hypertension and whose health was never robust, retreated to his laboratory in Surrey, seeking refuge in the relentless pursuit of invention. This private innovation was financed by the diminished but still existent resources of his company, driven by a deep personal need to prove that his vision encompassed not just the starting line of television, but its ultimate finish line as well. He aimed to jump straight to the next technological generation, determined to secure a position in the post-war world by demonstrating systems that rendered the 405-line standard obsolete even before it had fully established itself. This quiet, intense period saw some of his most profound and lasting technical contributions, proving that the electronic defeat had only redirected, not extinguished, his inventive fire.

10.2 Continuous Work on High-Definition Colour Television (The Telechrome Tube)

Having recognized that the future of home display technology belonged to the electronic cathode ray tube, Baird undertook a profound conceptual shift, transitioning from being a mechanical pioneer to an electronic innovator. His continuous work on colour television, dating back to his earliest successful experiments in 1928, now found its ultimate expression in an electronic solution: the invention of the Telechrome tube.

Baird's earliest colour television system, demonstrated almost a decade prior, was purely mechanical, relying on a spinning wheel containing red, green, and blue filters to sequentially illuminate the scene or analyze the projected image. While groundbreaking, this system was inherently flawed for high-definition due to its reliance on moving parts and the high speed of rotation required to prevent colour break-up. After 1937, Baird devoted himself to creating a fully electronic colour display that eliminated all mechanical components. The result was the Telechrome, a unique cathode ray tube designed to display colour images using an entirely non-mechanical, electronic principle.

The Telechrome tube, which was first publicly revealed during the war years, albeit under difficult circumstances, was fundamentally different from the shadow mask technology that would later become the global standard. Baird's design utilized a thin, semi-transparent sheet of mica or glass coated on both sides with different phosphors. One side might be coated with a green phosphor, and the other side with a blue-red combination. By controlling the voltage of the electron beam—its velocity—the beam could penetrate the mica sheet to varying degrees, exciting the phosphors on the front or the back, or both simultaneously, thus generating the required primary colours. Furthermore, Baird experimented with internal grids and screens to direct a single electron beam onto different coloured phosphor strips laid side-by-side.

This represented a staggering achievement: an attempt to generate a full-colour picture within a single electronic envelope. Although the resulting image was often dim and the colour registration was challenging to perfect, the Telechrome represented one of the most serious early attempts to solve the complex problem of electronic colour display. It was a revolutionary concept that prefigured the global drive for compatible, single-tube colour systems. By this time, the war had halted all civilian television development, meaning Baird's work was proceeding in a vacuum, without competition from his old rivals at EMI or from the rapidly advancing American firms.

The Telechrome system utilized a 600-line definition, significantly higher than the 405-line standard of the monochrome service, and used a dual-field system to transmit the colour information. While highly complex and requiring specialized receiving sets, the very existence of a working, all-electronic colour tube demonstrated Baird's ability to master the technology that had previously defeated him. His determination to jump ahead of the current monochrome standard was a powerful personal statement, proving that his inventive capabilities were focused not on preserving the past, but on realizing the ultimate potential of the medium. The colour television work of this period stands as Baird's final, and perhaps most technically complex, legacy.

10.3 The Development of Advanced Theatre Television (The Projector System)

One of the few commercially viable avenues left to the Baird Television Development Company after the Alexandra Palace defeat was large-screen projection, often referred to as theatre television. This application provided a crucial lifeline, demonstrating that Baird's electro-mechanical methods could still outperform purely electronic methods in specific high-power, large-scale roles. The limitations that doomed the mechanical system for home use—its complexity, size, and need for high illumination—were precisely the features necessary for projecting a large, bright image onto a cinema screen.

Baird's theatre television system, which saw a brief period of successful commercial operation, particularly at London's Dominion Theatre, relied on an advanced form of the Intermediate Film (IF) system. In this adaptation, live events, such as the Epsom Derby or important boxing matches, were captured by a standard film camera. The film was then rushed to a mobile IF processing unit, where it was developed, fixed, and scanned while still wet, a process that introduced a delay of about one minute. The signal, transmitted via radio link or high-frequency coaxial cable, was then used to modulate a powerful light source in the theatre.

Crucially, the theatre setup used a high-definition mirror-drum to physically project the image onto the cinema screen. This was not a passive display; it was a complex optical projector. The mirror-drum spun rapidly, reflecting the highly focused light from a powerful light source (often a high-intensity arc lamp) onto the screen, line by line. The high energy of the arc lamp, coupled with the efficiency of the mirror-drum, allowed for the projection of an image measuring up to fifteen by twelve feet—an astonishing size for the era—with a brightness and contrast unmatched by the early electronic projection methods being developed elsewhere.

The system was utilized successfully for a number of high-profile broadcasts in the late 1930s, proving that cinema audiences were willing to pay to watch distant live events in near real-time. This provided Baird's company with valuable revenue and maintained a visible presence in the public eye, even as the domestic market belonged entirely to EMI. The theatre television venture was a pragmatic compromise: it conceded the home market to electronics while asserting mechanical and electro-mechanical dominance in the large-screen projection niche. The high definition, often around 400 lines, demonstrated the potential of television as a mass entertainment medium in a shared venue, a concept that predated and eventually informed pay-per-view broadcasts. Although the outbreak of the Second World War abruptly halted this nascent industry, the large-screen projector system demonstrated Baird's ability to adapt his core technology to specialized, commercial applications, securing a final, tangible success for his engineers before the wartime blackout.

10.4 The Impact of the Second World War on Television Development in Britain

The outbreak of the Second World War in September 1939 brought civilian television development in Britain to an immediate and complete halt. The BBC television service, broadcasting from Alexandra Palace using the EMI-Marconi 405-line system, ceased transmission abruptly at the height of a Mickey Mouse cartoon, 'Mickey's Gala Premiere.' This sudden cessation was due to two major strategic concerns: firstly, the risk that the high-powered transmission signal would provide an excellent homing beacon for German bombers navigating towards London; and secondly, the need to immediately divert skilled engineers, critical electronic components, and vast financial resources to the war effort, particularly the rapidly developing field of radar.

The effect on the entire television industry was devastating, but for John Logie Baird and his company, the impact was arguably less disruptive to their technical direction than the 1937 defeat had been. Since they had already pivoted away from mainstream broadcast development, their primary projects—advanced colour systems and theatre television—were highly specialized and continued quietly. However, the war presented enormous logistical and personnel challenges. Key staff members were inevitably called up for military service or transferred to government defense work, leaving Baird with a significantly reduced team to continue his advanced research. The supply of crucial materials, particularly scarce electronic components and specialized glass for his experimental tubes, became extremely difficult, forcing the pace of development to slow dramatically.

Baird, whose health dictated that he remain in civilian life, moved his small laboratory operation away from the bomb-target risk of central London to his home in Bexhill-on-Sea, Sussex. Here, amidst the coastal blackouts and the constant threat of aerial attack, he continued his intense, personal drive for innovation. The atmosphere was one of grim determination. Research was focused, often narrowly, on achieving results with minimal resources. The war years were a period of isolation for Baird, cutting him off from the international exchange of scientific ideas, particularly the rapid electronic developments taking place in the United States. His focus remained fixed on high-definition colour and stereoscopy, driven by the belief that the post-war world would demand a system far superior to the pre-war 405-line monochrome standard.

Despite the hardships, the war provided an unexpected opportunity for reflection and theoretical work. Free from the commercial pressures of competing for a standard, Baird devoted significant time to writing technical papers and patent applications, rigorously documenting his complex ideas for future display and transmission systems. These documents, produced under the shadow of the conflict, represent a comprehensive intellectual legacy, proving that even while bombs fell, the inventive genius of the father of television was working tirelessly to define the medium's future, ensuring that the fruits of his private research would be ready for the moment peace returned and the television era recommenced.

10.5 Baird's Final Patented Inventions and Technical Documents from the War Years

The period from 1939 to 1945, though a time of global conflict and technological stagnation for public television, was surprisingly fertile for John Logie Baird's personal output of intellectual property. Cut off from external competition and resources, Baird concentrated on turning his complex ideas into formal patents and detailed technical documents, providing a clear blueprint for what he believed television should evolve into. These final patented inventions show an inventor dedicated not just to a higher definition, but to fundamentally changing the viewing experience through colour and depth.

Among his most significant final patents were those concerning extremely high-definition monochrome and colour systems. Recognizing the trend toward greater clarity, he patented systems for 600-line, 1,000-line, and even 2,000-line television. While these were entirely theoretical given the constraints of contemporary transmission technology, they demonstrated his future-forward thinking and the technical possibilities of his proposed scanning and display methods. These high-line count patents often relied on complex mechanical scanning at the transmitting end, paired with electronic display at the receiver, showing a continued faith in the efficiency of mechanical capture for high data rates.

Crucially, the patents filed during the war refined his electronic colour concepts, particularly the Telechrome tube and the principles of transmitting simultaneous colour information. His documentation moved away from the sequential field systems (where colour fields were sent one after the other) toward more complex, simultaneous transmission methods, which were technically challenging but necessary for compatibility with future high-speed standards. He continued to refine his stereoscopic, or three-dimensional, television, proposing systems that used alternating left and right-eye views synchronized with a rapidly rotating shutter or polarizing filters on the receiver, creating the illusion of depth. This work positioned him decades ahead of the general television industry's adoption of 3D technology.

Baird's technical documents from this time often took the form of detailed internal memos and comprehensive proposals to the government, anticipating the post-war reopening of the service. These papers argued passionately for the adoption of a much higher standard than the 405 lines, advocating for 600 or 1,000 lines, and making a strong case for colour. He saw the end of the war as a clean slate, a chance to bypass the technological compromises of the 1930s and jump straight to the truly high-fidelity future. His final papers, often written from his isolated coastal laboratory, represent the summation of his life's work—a detailed roadmap for the next generation of television technology. They demonstrate an enduring, prophetic vision for a medium that was to be defined by high-definition colour, large screens, and stereoscopic immersion, cementing his legacy as a relentless inventor whose ideas often ran far ahead of the commercial and engineering capabilities of his time. The tragedy of these final patents is that the inventor himself would not live to see their ultimate influence on the global television landscape.

Chapter 11: Personal Life, Health, and Family (1900–1946)

11.1 Marriage to Margaret Albu and the Dynamics of Family Life

For the first two decades of his inventive career, John Logie Baird was the quintessential solitary figure: a driven, often impoverished inventor living in damp, unheated workshops, his life dictated entirely by the demands of his current experiment and the endless pursuit of funding. This existence was not conducive to establishing personal stability, but in 1931, the trajectory of his private life shifted dramatically with his meeting of Margaret Albu. Margaret, a concert pianist originally from South Africa, offered a profound contrast to Baird's engineering-centric world. She was artistic, practical, and possessed a quiet strength that provided the necessary ballast to Baird's often chaotic and highly pressurized existence.

Their courtship was brief, and they married in November 1932. The marriage itself was perhaps an anomaly. By this time, Baird was the celebrated, if increasingly controversial, public face of British television. He was forty-four years old, frail in health, and deeply enmeshed in the demanding, high-stakes commercial battle against the electronic rivals. Margaret, though nine years his junior, brought a sense of order and emotional grounding that had been entirely absent from his prior life. She did not seek to understand the intricacies of Nipkow discs or cathode ray tubes, but she understood the man and the tremendous psychological pressure under which he labored.

The early years of their marriage were spent navigating the tempestuous financial and technical struggles of the Baird Television Development Company in London. They briefly settled in a house in Sydenham, a suburb that was a world away from the gritty Soho workshops of his pioneering days, but close enough to the engineering nerve centers of the capital. It was here that they began their family. Their first child,

Diana, was born in 1933, followed by a son, Malcolm, in 1935. This sudden establishment of a conventional family life placed extraordinary new demands on Baird, who was accustomed to prioritizing his inventions above all else, often neglecting his own basic needs.

Margaret's role evolved rapidly from wife to essential manager and shield. She took on the task of organizing their precarious domestic existence, protecting the fragile inventor from the constant demands of shareholders, reporters, and creditors. The financial instability of the company meant that their personal finances were never secure, even at the peak of the television boom. She managed the anxiety and stress of the household, ensuring that Baird had the necessary quiet and comfort to continue his work, especially as his persistent health issues worsened.

The family's move from London became necessary for two reasons: Baird's need for cleaner, sea air to combat his chronic illness, and the eventual outbreak of the Second World War. In 1940, they settled in the quiet coastal town of Bexhill-on-Sea in Sussex. This relocation effectively isolated Baird, allowing him to conduct his final, most advanced research—on colour and 3D television—in the enforced privacy of wartime isolation. It was within this stable, loving, yet often anxious family environment that Baird spent his final years, his immense intellectual drive sustained by the quiet presence of his wife and children, a stark contrast to the solitary bachelor struggling to make light dance in a distant attic room only a decade and a half prior. The family was his final, most enduring foundation.

11.2 Life in London and the Challenges of Chronic Illness (Tuberculosis)

The story of John Logie Baird's relentless inventive drive is inseparable from the chronic, debilitating health issues that plagued him throughout his life. From his early twenties, Baird suffered from severe and persistent illness, most significantly **tuberculosis**, or consumption, which was an ever-present factor shaping his choices, his career trajectory, and his working environment. His poor health fundamentally altered his educational path, forcing him to abandon his university studies in engineering prematurely, and subsequently drove his early, desperate search for warmer climates, believing the Scottish cold was a perpetual threat to his lungs.

The physical frailty did not diminish his mental acuity or his ambition; rather, it seemed to fuel a frantic urgency to achieve his goals before his time ran out. When he first began his serious television experiments in London and later in Hastings and back in London, his working conditions were notoriously Spartan. In the early 1920s, his workshop in Soho was often unheated, damp, and lacked proper ventilation—environments that were profoundly dangerous for a man suffering from pulmonary disease. Anecdotes from his early colleagues often recount Baird's gaunt appearance, his almost continuous physical exhaustion, and the necessity for him to take prolonged periods of rest to recuperate from bouts of illness. The sheer effort of maintaining a high-energy schedule of invention, company management, and public demonstration was a constant drain on his limited physical reserves.

This chronic condition instilled a unique rhythm in his work. He was capable of breathtaking bursts of concentrated, single-minded invention, working through nights and days until a breakthrough was made, only to be followed by inevitable physical collapse. This pattern of intense focus and enforced inactivity was deeply frustrating for the inventor but became the operational reality for his team and his family. The contrast between his fragile body and the colossal achievements emanating from his mind created a fascinating public image: the pale, quiet genius sacrificing his health for the sake of scientific progress.

The demands of the high-stakes high-definition trials in the mid-1930s put an even greater strain on him. The relentless travel, the negotiations, and the emotional toll of the Alexandra Palace defeat undoubtedly exacerbated his condition. Even the later financial pressures, which required him to be involved in endless boardroom arguments and patent filings, stole valuable energy from his diminishing reserves. The eventual move to Bexhill-on-Sea in 1940 was a necessary medical retreat as much as a response to the war. The cleaner air of the coast was intended to provide some therapeutic relief, allowing him to conserve his strength for his final, most complicated inventions in colour and 3D television. The battle against consumption was a lifelong, private war fought alongside his public battle for the future of broadcasting, defining both the urgency and the ultimate brevity of his revolutionary career.

11.3 Financial Struggles and the Stress of Perpetual Innovation

If chronic ill health was the physical adversary of John Logie Baird, then **financial instability** was the relentless commercial foe that dominated his entire adult life. Baird was a brilliant conceptual inventor and a tenacious engineer, but he possessed few, if any, business instincts. His early career was marked by a string of inventive schemes, from a specialized undersock to a glass razor, none of which resulted in lasting commercial success, teaching him little about sustainable enterprise. This pattern of brilliant invention followed by commercial failure repeated itself on a massive scale with television.

The Baird Television Development Company, despite being the pioneer in its field, was perpetually on the edge of insolvency. Television development, especially in the era of high-definition, was crushingly expensive, requiring specialized materials, large engineering teams, and substantial capital investment in complex machinery like the Intermediate Film apparatus and massive mirror-drums. Baird's company was never able to raise the kind of industrial capital or secure the comprehensive patent licensing enjoyed by his rival, the monolithic EMI-Marconi corporation. Instead, the company relied on a continuous cycle of attracting small-to-medium investors, often based purely on the spectacle of a demonstration or the promise of a future monopoly.

This reliance on venture capital meant that Baird was under constant, crippling pressure to produce results, often leading him to rush projects and make premature public claims that later damaged his credibility. He was forced to spend valuable time away from the laboratory, in boardrooms or on lecture tours, attempting to reassure increasingly restive shareholders. The greatest financial blow came in 1937 with the government's adoption of the EMI standard. The company stock collapsed, and the promise of national dominance—the sole commercial foundation of the firm—vanished overnight. The ensuing restructuring was brutal, confirming years of precarious financial management.

The stress this placed on Baird was immense. The burden of being personally responsible for the livelihoods of his loyal staff and the investments of hundreds of shareholders weighed heavily on him, exacerbating his fragile health. His final projects—colour and 3D television—were pursued not only out of scientific curiosity but out of a desperate, final hope that a technological leap could still redeem the company's fortunes and secure his family's future. Even after retreating to Bexhill, the financial anxieties persisted, forcing him to continue patenting and selling off intellectual property rights piecemeal to finance his ongoing, expensive private research. Baird never truly enjoyed the substantial financial rewards commensurate with his world-changing invention. His life was a testament to the high cost of pioneering a technology years before the commercial world was ready to support it, living his final years under the unrelenting strain of financial survival.

11.4 The Public Perception of Baird and his Relationship with the Press

Throughout his peak inventive years, John Logie Baird maintained a unique and often paradoxical relationship with the British press. In the 1920s, he was an instant **media sensation**, cast as the archetypal heroic inventor: the lone genius working against poverty and the skepticism of the scientific establishment. The press bestowed upon him romantic monikers such as the 'Wizard of Soho' and celebrated his humble, ingenious approach, often detailing the use of rudimentary materials like tea chests, biscuit tins, and darning needles in his first television apparatus. This romantic narrative captured the public imagination and was vital in attracting the early investment that kept his experiments afloat.

Baird, however, was fundamentally a shy, reserved, and private man. He possessed poor public speaking skills and an almost painful discomfort in the spotlight. This personality clashed sharply with the necessity of constant self-promotion required to sustain his company. He relied heavily on choreographed public demonstrations—the large-screen displays, the transatlantic transmission, the first colour images—to communicate his achievements. These events were meticulously managed to overcome the limitations of his actual broadcast technology, serving as crucial propaganda in the battle for public interest and capital.

The tone of the press coverage began to shift significantly in the early 1930s. As the limitations of the 30-line system became apparent and the sophisticated, well-funded electronic competition from EMI emerged, the initial adulation gave way to increasing skepticism. Reporters, once focused on the wonder of the invention, began to ask tougher questions about commercial viability, picture quality, and reliability. The contrast between the flickering images on the small home receiver and the clear, stable images demonstrated by EMI's electronic system was not lost on the technical journalists of the day.

The coverage of the Alexandra Palace trials in 1936-1937 was the culmination of this changing relationship. The press reported the competition fairly, detailing the technical advantages of the EMI system and the operational failures of the Baird system. While Baird was still treated with respect as the great pioneer, the narrative shifted to one of technological progress overriding historical achievement. He became a figure of transition—a man of the past facing the future.

During the isolated war years, Baird's public profile diminished further. He was still recognized as the 'father of television,' but his work on 600-line colour and 3D was often relegated to short, academic footnotes in the newspapers, overshadowed by the intense focus on the war effort and radar development. Yet, despite the commercial defeat and the eventual technological obsolescence of his initial systems, Baird's place in the public memory as the man who first transmitted a moving image remained permanent. This legacy, secured by those early dramatic headlines, ensured that his name was forever synonymous with the birth of television, a testament to the power of a single, highly publicized moment of invention.

11.5 Baird as a Mentor and the Team of Engineers Who Worked Closely with Him

John Logie Baird, while the undisputed visionary behind the entire enterprise, was never a solitary inventor in the final decades of his career. The scale and complexity of high-definition television demanded a highly competent and dedicated team of engineers, technicians, and chemists. Baird's leadership style was unique, characterized by an infectious enthusiasm and an almost total devotion to the inventive process, but also by a lack of consistent, managerial structure, which sometimes led to chaos in the laboratory.

The men who worked for him, such as his chief engineer T.H. Bridgewater and later colleagues like G. V. Holt and J. C. Wilson, were drawn not by guaranteed salary or job security—which the company certainly could not offer—but by the sheer excitement of working at the absolute cutting edge of technology under the world's most famous inventor. They were intensely loyal to Baird the man, even if they sometimes privately questioned the viability of his mechanical principles. The laboratories of the Baird Company were known for their atmosphere of frantic, rapid prototyping, where ingenuity and quick fixes were celebrated, and the use of unconventional, often low-cost, materials was common. It was an inventor's workshop first and a corporation second.

Baird served less as a traditional manager and more as a spiritual and conceptual mentor. He would present a seemingly impossible problem—such as how to project a 240-line image onto a cinema screen or how to create a single tube for colour—and then step back, allowing his engineers the intellectual freedom to develop the solution, often using his own core ideas as a starting point. This hands-on, problem-solving environment fostered incredible creativity.

The greatest test of this mentorship was the technical shift imposed by the rise of electronics. Many of Baird's core team eventually had to reconcile their loyalty to the pioneer with the evident technological superiority of the electronic path. This tension was fruitful: Baird's later, most advanced work, such as the 600-line **Telechrome** colour tube, was not developed by Baird alone but was the result of his engineering team successfully persuading him to abandon mechanical scanning entirely for the display side and embrace the electronic cathode ray tube. His acceptance of the Telechrome marked the ultimate trust in his team's judgment and the maturation of his own inventive perspective.

The loyalty of this small group proved essential during the war years. After the company's mainstream defeat and the move to Bexhill, only a handful of dedicated engineers remained with Baird. They maintained the complex, experimental colour and 3D systems in isolation, working through supply shortages and under wartime constraints. It was their collective effort, driven by Baird's enduring vision, that allowed him to demonstrate the world's first all-electronic colour television picture in 1944. This final, profound achievement stands as a testament not only to Baird's persistence but to the dedication and brilliance of the team he inspired and mentored throughout the turbulent years of his final innovative push.

Chapter 12: Legacy and Final Assessments (1946–Present)

12.1 Death in Bexhill-on-Sea, Sussex, and the Immediate Tributes

John Logie Baird's life of relentless invention and chronic illness reached its close shortly after the end of the war that had both isolated him and spurred his final, most advanced research. On June 14, 1946, at the age of fifty-seven, he died at his home in Bexhill-on-Sea, Sussex, following a cerebral hemorrhage. His death was quiet, a marked contrast to the high-voltage public career he had pursued for two decades, and it occurred just as the world began to anticipate the return of peacetime broadcasting. His death was not entirely unexpected by those close to him, given his long history of debilitating illness, including tuberculosis, which had shadowed him since his youth and left him physically frail.

The news of his passing immediately triggered a wave of tributes, both in Britain and internationally, confirming his unique and pivotal status. The obituaries universally recognized him as the **father of television**, a title that transcended the technical arguments of the 1930s. Newspapers across the country dedicated significant space to recounting the romantic story of the solitary Scottish inventor who, working with rudimentary materials in a dingy London attic, had first succeeded in transmitting a moving image. The emphasis was overwhelmingly placed on his pioneering status—the first successful demonstration of television in 1926, the first transatlantic broadcast in 1928, and the establishment of the world's first public television service in 1929. The public memory focused on the triumph of the initial concept, rather than the subsequent commercial and technical struggles against electronic systems.

The BBC, which had defeated his system a decade prior, offered respectful and lengthy tributes, acknowledging their debt to his foundational work. Engineers, even those who had worked on the rival electronic system, spoke of his genius and tenacity. The prevailing sentiment was one of profound respect for his sheer inventive spirit. His former colleagues emphasized his vision for colour and 3D television, systems he had been refining privately until his death. These tributes underscored the belief that Baird's failure to secure the long-term commercial standard was a result of his being ahead of his time, and that his mechanical methods, while ultimately superseded, were necessary to demonstrate the fundamental feasibility of the technology when electronic components were still immature.

The immediate assessment of Baird's legacy was thus highly generous, placing him firmly in the pantheon of great British inventors alongside figures like Stephenson and Faraday. His burial in the family plot in Helensburgh, Scotland, brought his life full circle, connecting the great innovator back to the quiet, academic roots of his beginnings. The tributes acknowledged the financial and physical sacrifices he had made, painting him as a martyr to his own scientific curiosity.

12.2 The Debate: Mechanical Genius vs. Electronic Failure

The decades following John Logie Baird's death saw his historical assessment solidify into a complex, bifurcated debate among historians and engineers: was he a mechanical genius whose persistence made television possible, or was he a technological conservative who failed to recognize the future belonged to electronics? This debate centers on the period between 1930 and 1937, the critical years when the low-definition 30-line mechanical system was challenged and ultimately replaced by the high-definition 405-line electronic system.

The "mechanical genius" argument holds that Baird was an **enabling pioneer**. Proponents of this view argue that without his tireless efforts, television might have remained a theoretical concept for many years longer. His use of the Nipkow disc and mechanical scanning systems, while crude, allowed him to create a working television set using the technology available in the 1920s—photoelectric cells, neon lamps, and simple amplification. His early successes forced the hands of governments and large corporations, proving television was viable and thereby accelerating the enormous investment required to develop the superior electronic cathode ray tube systems. In this sense, his mechanical apparatus was the essential **scaffolding** upon which the electronic industry was built. He solved the core problem of sequential picture transmission and reception.

Conversely, the "electronic failure" critique focuses on his later intransigence and his defeat at Alexandra Palace. Critics argue that Baird's intense, almost sentimental attachment to mechanical principles blinded him to the obvious superiority of electronic scanning, which offered vastly higher resolution, stability, and light output without the inherent noise and vibration of moving parts. They point to his company's costly commitment to complex Intermediate Film and mirror-drum apparatuses, resources that could have been better directed toward electronic research. This view suggests that he became a historical footnote because he resisted the necessary technological transition, allowing EMI-Marconi to seize the standard and dominate the industry.

However, a more nuanced assessment suggests the debate itself is flawed, recognizing Baird as a **transitional figure** whose entire career was a bridge between the electro-mechanical and the electronic worlds. His final, most advanced work—the electronic Telechrome colour tube and high-definition electronic projector systems—demonstrates that he ultimately mastered the electronic technologies that had initially defeated him. By the time of his death, he was designing all-electronic colour systems superior to the existing monochrome standard. Therefore, his failure was not one of vision or even of technical capability in the end, but primarily one of *corporate scale and financial capital*. He was a small, inventor-led company competing against a global industrial powerhouse. His ultimate place in history is cemented as the crucial figure who *proved* television could work, thereby charting the course for all subsequent development.

12.3 Post-War Recognition and the Resumption of British Television

The resumption of the British television service in 1946, following the six-year wartime blackout, served as an immediate, if painful, reminder of John Logie Baird's absence and the final verdict on his mechanical system. When the BBC broadcast returned from Alexandra Palace, it recommenced using the same EMI-Marconi 405-line standard it had abruptly switched off in 1939. This established standard, now firmly entrenched as the national system, permanently confirmed the electronic route as the foundation of British broadcasting for the next few decades.

Despite the technical defeat, the post-war era brought Baird considerable **formal recognition**. The government and professional engineering bodies increasingly acknowledged the magnitude of his foundational achievement. His legacy was honored through the naming of scholarships, scientific prizes, and memorial plaques. More importantly, the patents and technical blueprints Baird had meticulously compiled during the war years, particularly those concerning colour and stereoscopic television, provided crucial reference points for future researchers. His work on the Telechrome tube, for instance, informed discussions about the shape and challenges of future colour systems, even though the specific technology was not adopted.

The cultural impact of Baird's pioneering spirit intensified in the decades following his death. As television ownership soared in the 1950s and 1960s, public interest in the medium's origins grew, and Baird's story—the man who invented it—became firmly woven into the national narrative of technological innovation. He was not just a name; he was the symbol of British ingenuity.

This legacy was particularly potent in his native Scotland, where he became a source of immense national pride. Educational institutions and museums dedicated resources to documenting his life, ensuring that his role as the true inventor of working television was never overlooked by the focus on the electronic revolution that followed. Post-war recognition also extended to his family, who, despite years of financial hardship, finally saw the public and historical validation of Baird's immense sacrifices. The debate over whether he chose the right technology was increasingly supplanted by the consensus that he was the right man at the right time to kickstart the age of electronic visual communication. His work provided the proof of concept that launched one of the most transformative technologies of the twentieth century, and the post-war world, finally enjoying the medium he created, afforded him the stature he had always deserved.

12.4 Preserving the Artifacts: Televisors and Phonovision Records in Museums

A critical aspect of John Logie Baird's enduring legacy is the physical preservation of his early artifacts, which serve as tangible proof of his pioneering achievement. Unlike many early inventors whose work exists only in documentation, Baird's early mechanical systems, known as Televisors, and the unique sound recordings of early broadcasts, known as Phonovision records, offer direct physical evidence of the birth of television. These items are now invaluable museum pieces, central to the history of technology.

The **Baird Televisor**, the mechanical receiver sold to the public in the late 1920s and early 1930s, is perhaps the most iconic of these artifacts. Featuring a small window through which the 30-line image was viewed, and requiring the user to look directly at the spinning Nipkow disc, these early devices are now housed in major collections, including the Science Museum in London and museums in Scotland. Their preservation allows visitors to grasp the rudimentary nature of the medium at its inception and appreciate the magnitude of the subsequent technological leap. These Televisors, despite their technical obsolescence, stand as the first commercially available television receivers in the world.

Even more significant from a historical perspective are the **Phonovision records**. These were gramophone records Baird used to store and replay the fragile 30-line television signals. In the earliest days, video recording technology did not exist, so Baird ingeniously adapted audio recording to capture the low-frequency video signals. The resulting grooves on the record, which appear normal to the eye, actually encode the flickering images. These records are extraordinarily difficult to decode, requiring specialized playback equipment to convert the audio track back into a discernible image. The successful recovery and analysis of some of these records, particularly the footage of the famous "Stookie Bill" ventriloquist doll, provide the world with the only surviving images of the very first public television broadcasts.

The preservation of these artifacts is not merely an academic exercise; it is the ultimate vindication of Baird's claims. The Phonovision records directly refute the skepticism of those who doubted the efficacy of the 30-line system, offering irrefutable proof that a moving, synchronized picture was indeed being transmitted and recorded in the 1920s. Museums and institutions have invested heavily in restoring and cataloging these items, ensuring that future generations can witness the literal dawn of broadcasting. The artifacts themselves, from the rudimentary Televisor to the mysterious grooves of the Phonovision records, serve as powerful reminders that every technological revolution begins with a crude, working prototype, and that Baird's genius lay in creating the first such device that mattered.

12.5 Baird's Enduring Place in History as the Inventor of the First Working Television

John Logie Baird's enduring place in history is secured by the single, crucial fact that he invented and publicly demonstrated the **first working television system**. This is a distinction that remains largely uncontested among serious historians of technology, defining his position regardless of the subsequent evolutionary paths the technology took. His achievement was not just the theoretical proposition of television, which had been explored since the late 19th century, but the crucial engineering feat of combining existing components—from scanning discs to photo-electric cells—into a functional, end-to-end communication system.

The phrase "first working television" is precise and important. It refers to the successful public demonstration on January 26, 1926, at his laboratory in London, before members of the Royal Institution and a press representative. This demonstration was the world's first true television system capable of transmitting and receiving moving images with gradations of light and shade—not merely silhouettes. This event marks the true beginning of the medium and the transition of television from science fiction to scientific reality.

Baird's legacy also stands as a potent symbol of **individual genius versus corporate power**. His story represents the classic battle between the isolated, often self-funded inventor and the massive, institutionalized industrial research laboratory. While he lost the battle for the *standard* to the superior resources and electronic technology of EMI-Marconi, he forever won the historical claim to the *creation*. This narrative adds a human, romantic element to the history of a complex technology, ensuring his name resonates culturally in a way that corporate names often do not.

Furthermore, his final, advanced research secured his reputation as a visionary. His work on all-electronic colour systems, high-definition standards of up to 2,000 lines, and stereoscopic television confirmed that his vision extended far beyond the limitations of his initial mechanical devices. He was a man who saw the ultimate potential of television—an interactive, high-fidelity, and immersive medium—and worked tirelessly to realize it, even after his initial system had been surpassed.

In the final analysis, Baird's immense historical importance is not that his technology survived, but that his success initiated the technological race. He was the catalyst. He moved the entire field of visual electronic communication past the initial threshold of possibility, setting the stage for the electronic giants that followed. The legacy of John Logie Baird is thus one of foundational brilliance, relentless struggle, and a pioneering spirit that ultimately defined the age of mass visual communication. He started the whole show, and for that, his name will forever be etched at the beginning of television history.

Conclusion

The Singular Contribution: Television's Foundational Architect

The life and work of John Logie Baird represent one of the most compelling narratives in the history of modern technology, a story of singular vision and relentless execution that transitioned a long-cherished scientific dream into a global reality. Baird's contribution to global communication is not merely that he was one of many working on the problem of visual transmission; rather, his distinction lies in being the first individual in human history to successfully complete the **end-to-end communication chain of television**. It was his apparatus, however crude, that first demonstrated to the world, on January 26, 1926, that it was scientifically and technically possible to capture a moving image, translate it into electrical signals, transmit those signals, and then reassemble them into a recognizable picture at a distance. This achievement represents a fundamental paradigm shift, moving the concept of *tele-vision* from the realm of theoretical physics and scattered patent applications into the tangible sphere of applied engineering.

Before Baird, the transmission of moving images was an elegant but unproven concept, reliant on the theoretical potential of components like the Nipkow disc. It was Baird who took these disparate ideas and, through sheer tenacity and inventive dexterity, hammered them into a functioning, verifiable system. His initial apparatus—famously cobbled together from simple materials like tea chests, darning needles, and biscuit tins—was a perfect reflection of his resourceful, pioneering spirit. While critics often focus on the simplicity and eventual obsolescence of his low-definition, 30-line mechanical system, they often overlook the enormous complexity of the core problem he solved: synchronisation. For a television system to work, the rapidly scanning mechanism at the transmitter must operate in perfect lockstep with the recreating mechanism at the receiver. Achieving this stability, even with a flicker-prone, monochrome image, was an engineering triumph of the highest order, requiring an understanding of optics, physics, electronics, and mechanical precision.

Baird's singular contribution extends far beyond that pivotal moment in 1926. He was also the architect of nearly every subsequent technological landmark in the early history of the medium. He was responsible for the **first transatlantic television broadcast** in 1928, physically bridging the continents with a visual signal, a feat that shocked the world and firmly established his international reputation. More remarkably, he was the first to demonstrate **colour television** and **stereoscopic (3D) television**, doing so decades before either technology became commercially viable. His 1928 demonstration of a three-colour image—created using spinning discs with coloured filters—was a powerful testament to his vision, proving that the medium was not limited to monochrome. He saw television not just as a replacement for radio, but as a vehicle for fully immersive visual experience, encompassing depth and hue. These achievements demonstrate that Baird was not simply a relic of the mechanical age; he was a true visionary who mapped out the full potential of the medium, even though the necessary electronic tools to realize that potential were not yet fully mature.

The establishment of the **world's first public television service** by the BBC using Baird's 30-line system in 1929 solidified his place as the founder of the broadcasting age. Though the service was small and limited, it was operational, broadcasting regular programmes and establishing the crucial administrative and technical frameworks that all subsequent television broadcasters would follow. His work provided the initial commercial impetus, the excitement, and the necessary proof of concept that compelled governments and major corporations around the world, most notably in the United States, Germany, and

Russia, to accelerate their own television research. Baird was, therefore, the essential catalyst. He was the force that turned a quiet scientific theory into a frenetic global industrial race, forever changing the landscape of human communication and ushering in an era where the simultaneous transmission of image and sound became a ubiquitous fact of modern life. His legacy is embedded not just in museums, but in the very fabric of how the modern world shares news, culture, and entertainment.

The Persistence of the Pioneer: Proving the Concept

The narrative of John Logie Baird is fundamentally a study in **persistence in the face of overwhelming adversity**. His life was a protracted, agonizing battle waged on multiple fronts: against debilitating chronic illness, against relentless financial insolvency, and ultimately, against the technological tide of the superior electronic systems developed by vast industrial rivals. It was this sheer, unyielding tenacity, more than any single technical blueprint, that ensured television's feasibility and permanence.

Baird's fight began with his health. Afflicted by chronic illness, most notably tuberculosis, his physical resources were constantly depleted. Yet, this frailty seemed only to intensify his intellectual urgency. Knowing his time was likely limited, he pursued his inventions with a desperate, almost manic energy, driving himself and his small team through impossible hours. His ability to work in bursts of intense creativity, interspersed with periods of enforced recovery, created a unique rhythm in his life. This was not the persistence of a sturdy, corporate research team, but the single-minded focus of an individual driven by a profound and personal race against time. The fact that he achieved so much while battling such a persistent physical adversary is perhaps the most impressive measure of his personal fortitude.

The commercial obstacles were equally daunting. Baird was, by nature, an inventor, not a businessman, and his company, the Baird Television Development Company, was chronically undercapitalized. Throughout the 1920s and 1930s, the company existed in a perpetual state of financial stress, reliant on the sporadic injections of capital secured through dramatic public demonstrations and the enthusiasm of speculative investors. This financial instability forced Baird into a relentless cycle of self-promotion, requiring him to take time away from his laboratory to reassure shareholders, give lectures, and engage the press. His persistence here was not in the laboratory, but in the boardroom and on the stage—maintaining the belief and the funding necessary to keep his expensive experiments alive. Had Baird lacked this entrepreneurial stubbornness, the early service would have collapsed years before the BBC was ready to commit to any form of television.

The ultimate test of his persistence came with the **Alexandra Palace competition** in the mid-1930s. Faced with the evident technical superiority of the EMI-Marconi electronic system, Baird's response was not surrender, but intensified innovation. He and his team spent enormous amounts of effort attempting to perfect their mechanical system, employing complex mirror-drums and Intermediate Film technology in a desperate attempt to match the electronic picture quality. While he ultimately lost the standard, his subsequent work during the isolation of the Second World War proves the enduring nature of his spirit. Retreating to Bexhill-on-Sea, and stripped of the pressures of running a major company, Baird focused entirely on pure research. It was here that his persistence paid off in its final, intellectual form: he developed and demonstrated an all-electronic, high-definition colour television picture using his Telechrome tube. This final triumph—mastering the very electronic technology that had defeated his mechanical system—underscored that his failure was never one of vision or intellectual capability, but merely one of timing and capital. His persistence ensured that, even in defeat, he pointed the way to the television's electronic future.

Final Assessment: Triumph of the Spirit

John Logie Baird's legacy rests upon a final assessment that moves beyond the simplistic dichotomy of mechanical genius versus electronic failure. He was the necessary bridge, the crucial interim figure who, by making the impossible tangible, fundamentally reshaped the trajectory of global communication. The true value of his pioneering spirit lies in his ability to seize an established theoretical challenge and transform it into a demonstrable, working piece of technology using the components of his time. This is the definition of the pioneering inventor: one who makes the first successful crossing, clearing the path for those with superior vehicles to follow.

His defeat at Alexandra Palace in 1937 was not a failure of innovation, but a natural and inevitable consequence of the technological evolutionary curve. Baird's great success was building the world's first working television with 1920s technology; his great struggle was trying to compete with 1930s technology developed by industrial giants with unlimited capital. History is replete with examples of the pioneers whose initial, rough inventions are quickly superseded by more refined versions. George Stephenson's early locomotives were replaced by superior designs, and Guglielmo Marconi's initial primitive wireless systems gave way to more sophisticated radio technology. Yet, all three men hold the unassailable claim to being the **founder of their respective fields**. Baird belongs in this rarefied company.

The enduring impact of Baird's life is his powerful representation of the individual against the institution. His story embodies the classic, romantic archetype of the inventor: the solitary genius driven by a consuming vision, sacrificing personal comfort and physical health for the sake of an idea. This human element is what makes the Baird narrative so powerful. Unlike the corporate research teams at RCA or

EMI, Baird was the face and the sole driving force of his invention. He mortgaged his life and health for television, and this personal sacrifice resonates far more deeply than the collective work of an anonymous laboratory.

In the final assessment, John Logie Baird was a relentless visionary who refused to let his limitations—be they physical, commercial, or technological—define his success. He started the television revolution, not only by showing that moving images could be transmitted, but also by demonstrating that the future of broadcasting lay in colour and 3D. While the specific components he championed did not survive the war, his vision did. He proved the viability of the medium and accelerated its arrival by decades, forever changing how humanity experiences events, shares culture, and perceives the world. His pioneering spirit triumphed over every daunting obstacle, and for that, he will always be remembered as the true, foundational architect of global visual communication.

Appendix

List of Key Patents (1923–1946)

John Logie Baird's relentless pursuit of television technology resulted in a significant number of patents, reflecting the breadth of his inventive scope, from the fundamental mechanical apparatus to early forms of colour and large-screen display. The patents listed below represent key milestones in the development of his system and its subsequent innovations.

- **GB222604 (1923) – Improvements in apparatus for transmitting views or images to a distance:** This is the foundational patent covering Baird's initial mechanical scanning system, relying on the use of lenses and perforations on a rotating disc (the Nipkow principle) to dissect and synthesize an image. It covers the core concept of scanning the object directly with light, which was crucial for his early low-definition demonstrations.
- **GB230576 (1924) – Improvements in and relating to the transmission of views, scenes or images to a distance:** This patent expands on the basic transmission system, detailing methods for achieving synchronisation between the transmitter and receiver, a critical hurdle in making television practical. It describes using electrical impulses derived from the scanning mechanism itself.
- **GB237936 (1924) – Improvements in apparatus for the electrical transmission of views, scenes, or images:** Focusing on the receiving end, this patent covers the design of the display device, including the use of a modified neon lamp whose light intensity could be modulated rapidly by the incoming electrical signal to reconstruct the image.
- **GB282855 (1927) – Improvements in the method of and

apparatus for the transmission of views, scenes, or images to a distance: A vital patent that covers Baird's work on **colour television.** It describes a system using three scanning devices (or a single device with three sets of spirals) combined with colour filters (red, green, and blue) at both the transmitting and receiving ends to achieve sequential colour transmission.

- **GB289108 (1927) – Apparatus for stereoscopic television:** This patent details Baird's method for transmitting and receiving **three-dimensional images.** It involved alternating the view from two slightly offset lenses at the transmitter and presenting the alternating images to the receiver, where viewers used a synchronized viewer (similar to a stereo viewer) to perceive depth.
- **GB315357 (1928) – Improvements in and relating to television apparatus:** This covers the development of his earliest forms of **large-screen television**, often achieved using an array of small light sources (like miniature electric bulbs or neon tubes) that were sequentially illuminated and modulated to create a composite, larger image visible to a crowd.
- **GB336829 (1929) – Television apparatus:** Describes improvements to the scanning process, particularly related to the use of a mirror drum instead of a simple Nipkow disc for higher definition scanning, moving towards the more sophisticated mechanical systems used in the BBC service.
- **GB406324 (1932) – Improvements in and relating to television and like apparatus:** Covers the concept of **Intermediate Film (IF) television**, a hybrid system where the scene was rapidly filmed, the film developed instantly, and then scanned electronically or mechanically while still wet.

This was an attempt to overcome the light sensitivity problems of early live scanning.

- **GB564344 (1943) – Improvements in and relating to cathode-ray tubes for television and the like:** A highly significant later patent concerning **all-electronic colour television**. This relates to his "Telechrome" display tube, a fully electronic solution that used two fluorescent screens coated with different phosphors (orange-red and blue-green) and viewed at an angle, representing his final leap into electronic systems.

Glossary of Technical Terms

The early history of television is filled with specialized terms, many of which are associated directly with Baird's mechanical system. Understanding these terms is essential to appreciate the technical environment in which he worked.

- **Nipkow Disc (or Scanning Disk):** The fundamental component of early mechanical television. Invented by Paul Nipkow in 1884, it is a flat, rotating disk with a spiral pattern of small holes or apertures. As the disc rotates, the holes sequentially scan the image area, breaking it down into a series of light pulses. Baird's earliest successful apparatus used a Nipkow disc.

- **Scanning:** The process of converting an image into an electrical signal by systematically analyzing the brightness of the image elements, line by line. In mechanical television, this was done by the Nipkow disc; in electronic television, it is done by an electron beam.

- **Resolution (Lines):** The measure of detail in a television picture, defined by the number of horizontal lines scanned. Baird's earliest public demonstrations used a **30-line** system, which was considered low-definition. The BBC public service began with 30 lines before moving to 240 lines (Baird's mechanical system) and eventually the high-definition electronic standard of 405 lines.

- **Televisor:** The trade name given to Baird's mechanical television receiver, first sold commercially in the late 1920s. It typically housed a Nipkow disc and a neon lamp, allowing the user to view the received image through a magnifying lens.

- **Phonovision:** Baird's system for recording television signals onto conventional gramophone records for later playback. Demonstrated in 1927, this was the world's first form of recorded video, albeit at very low quality.

- **Selenium Cell:** A photoelectric cell used in early television cameras. When light struck the selenium, its electrical resistance changed, converting the varying light intensity into a fluctuating electrical signal that could be transmitted. It was essential to Baird's earliest successful image capture.
- **Neon Lamp (or Neon Tube):** Used in the **Televisor** receiver. This lamp glows when an electrical current passes through it. By modulating the current based on the incoming television signal, Baird could vary the light output of the lamp, recreating the brightness of the scanned image point-by-point.
- **Intermediate Film (IF) Television:** A complex, high-speed, hybrid system developed by Baird to achieve better picture quality and light sensitivity. It involved rapidly filming the scene (often at 17 frames per second), developing the film in a continuous chemical bath inside the camera, and then scanning the still-wet film using a high-definition mechanical scanner before it was discarded.
- **Mirror Drum:** A sophisticated mechanical scanning device, typically a cylinder with a series of small mirrors mounted around its circumference at slightly varying angles. When rotated rapidly, the mirror drum could achieve a higher number of scanning lines (up to 240 in the Baird system) than the simpler Nipkow disc.
- **Telechrome:** Baird's final major invention, an **all-electronic colour cathode-ray tube** developed during the Second World War. It used a flat screen with phosphors arranged to display colour, representing his full acceptance and successful application of electronic principles, years after his mechanical

system was superseded.

Timeline of Major Milestones

This timeline charts the critical moments in John Logie Baird's career, from his early life to his major inventions and the public launch of television broadcasting.

- **1888, August 13:** John Logie Baird is born in Helensburgh, Dunbartonshire, Scotland, the youngest son of a Free Church of Scotland minister.
- **1915:** Graduates from the Royal Technical College in Glasgow (now the University of Strathclyde) and begins working, his education interrupted by bouts of illness.
- **1923:** Moves to Hastings, England, focusing exclusively on developing television. Files his first fundamental patent for the transmission of images.
- **1924, February:** Achieves his first successful transmission of a silhouette (outline) image over a short distance.
- **1925, October 2:** Achieves the first successful transmission of a recognizable **grayscale human face** (that of his office boy, William Taynton) at the Selfridges department store in London. This is often considered the first true television image.
- **1926, January 26:** Gives the world's first public demonstration of true television—the transmission of moving images with tone gradation—to members of the Royal Institution in his London laboratory. The resolution is 30 lines.
- **1927, May:** Demonstrates **Phonovision**, recording television signals onto gramophone discs.
- **1927, May:** The Baird Television Development Company is formed.

- **1928, July:** Achieves the world's first demonstration of **colour television** using spinning discs and filters.
- **1928, August:** Achieves the world's first demonstration of **stereoscopic (3D) television**.
- **1928, September:** Achieves the **first transatlantic television transmission**, sending a signal from London to Hartsdale, New York.
- **1917, November:** The BBC begins experimental television broadcasts using the Baird 30-line system from its London studio. This marks the beginning of the **world's first public television service**.
- **1930:** The first televised play, *The Man with the Flower in His Mouth*, is broadcast by the BBC using the Baird system.
- **1932:** Baird demonstrates the Intermediate Film system in an effort to improve picture quality.
- **1936, November:** The BBC inaugurates the world's first regular, high-definition public television service from Alexandra Palace. The service alternates weekly between the 240-line Baird mechanical system and the 405-line EMI-Marconi electronic system.
- **1937, February:** The BBC officially drops the Baird mechanical system in favour of the technically superior, all-electronic EMI-Marconi system.
- **1939, September 1:** The BBC television service is abruptly suspended at the outbreak of the Second World War. Baird continues independent research throughout the war years.
- **1944, August:** Baird demonstrates a fully electronic, high-definition **600-line colour television system** using his Telechrome tube.
- **1946, June 14:** John Logie Baird dies in Bexhill-on-Sea, Sussex, England, at the age of 57.

Bibliographical Notes and Source Suggestions

A thorough study of John Logie Baird requires consulting primary source documents—patents, contemporary technical journals, and autobiographical writings—as well as comprehensive secondary sources that offer balanced historical perspective.

Primary Sources and Baird's Own Account

- **Baird, John Logie. *Sermons, Soap and Television*. London: Royal Television Society, 1988 (posthumous publication of his autobiography):** This is the essential primary source. Written largely during the war years, it provides a direct, often witty, and highly personal account of his struggles and triumphs, particularly the early years of poverty and his first experiments. It is invaluable for understanding his mindset and persistence.
- **Contemporary Technical Journals (e.g., *Wireless World*, *Nature*, *The Electrician*):** These journals contain the critical technical papers and reports written by Baird and his engineers detailing the specifications of his systems (30-line, mirror drum, Intermediate Film) and the initial reports on his groundbreaking public demonstrations (1926, 1928 transatlantic, 1928 colour).
- **Patent Archives:** Reviewing the original patent specifications (listed above) provides the most precise technical details of his inventions and the claims he made for them, showcasing the evolution of his ideas.

Key Secondary Sources and Biographies

- **Burns, Russell.** *John Logie Baird: Television Pioneer.* **London: The Institution of Electrical Engineers, 2000:** Considered one of the most authoritative and technically rigorous biographies. Burns provides a balanced assessment of Baird's achievements against his corporate and electronic rivals, offering detailed explanations of the mechanical systems.
- **Moseley, Sydney A.** *John Baird: The Romance and Tragedy of the Inventor.* **London: Europa Publications, 1935:** Written during Baird's lifetime by his personal publicist, this book is more of a contemporary promotional piece but offers vivid, first-hand anecdotes and a sense of the public excitement and financial pressures surrounding Baird's work in the 1920s and early 1930s.
- **O'Neill, Bill.** *John Logie Baird: A Life.* **London: John Murray, 1990:** A well-regarded, accessible modern biography that attempts to capture the cultural and personal dimensions of Baird's life alongside his technical work.
- **Abramson, Albert.** *The History of Television, 1880 to 1941.* **Jefferson, NC: McFarland, 1987:** An essential general history of television that places Baird's work in the broader context of global electronic development, providing crucial details on his competitors (e.g., Farnsworth, Zworykin, EMI-Marconi).

Source Suggestions for Further Research

- **The Archives of the BBC:** Contain documents relating to the establishment and eventual discontinuation of the 30-line and 240-line Baird services at Alexandra Palace.
- **The National Museum of Scotland (Edinburgh):** Holds key

artifacts, including surviving pieces of Baird's original apparatus.
- **Academic Studies on Media Technology:** Articles and papers published by media historians that analyze the cultural impact of early broadcasting and the transition from mechanical to electronic television. These sources are useful for exploring the societal excitement and business challenges of the era.

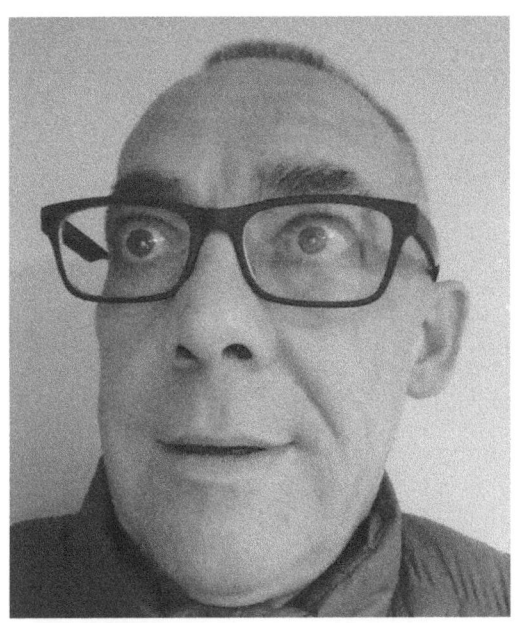

About the Author

Born and raised in a small town on the east coast of Scotland, the author brings a unique and refreshing voice to his writing. A late-in-life diagnosis of Asperger's Syndrome illuminated his lifelong journey, giving him a deeper understanding of the distinct way he sees the world.

Describing himself as an optimist on a mission to entertain and inform, he aims to take the reader's imagination to its limits and deliver a truly unforgettable experience.

www.ingramcontent.com/pod-product-compliance
Ingram Content Group UK Ltd.
Pitfield, Milton Keynes, MK11 3LW, UK
UKHW010634270126
10336UKWH00027B/120